Nudibranchs

of Britain, Ireland and Northwest Europe

Second Edition

Bernard Picton and Christine Morrow

WILD NATURE PRESS

PRINCETON

We would like to dedicate this book to our dear friend and dive buddy Erling Svensen, for the contribution he has made to bringing the beauty and diversity of our underwater marine life to so many people through his outstanding and inspirational photography.

Published by Princeton University Press
41 William Street, Princeton, New Jersey 08540
99 Banbury Road, Oxford OX2 6JX
press.princeton.edu

British Library Cataloging-in-Publication Data is available

Library of Congress Control Number 2023932473
ISBN 978-0-691-20879-4
Ebook ISBN 978-0-691-23069-6

Series Publisher Julie Dando,
WILDNATUREPRESS Ltd., Plymouth

Printed in Italy

10 9 8 7 6 5 4 3 2 1

Front cover: *Fjordia browni* feeding on *Tubularia indivisa*, Gulen, Norway.
Back cover: top left, *Tritonia hombergii*, Skau, Nordland, Norway; top right, *Jorunna artsdatabankia*, The Maidens, Northern Ireland; middle left, *Antiopella cristata*, Skomer Island, Wales; middle right, *Fjordia chriskaugei*, Gulen Norway; bottom left: *Polycera quadrilineata*, orange spotted form, Gulen, Norway; bottom right: *Hero formosa*, Gulen, Norway.

Contents

Acknowledgements

The in situ photos used in this book are the accumulation of countless diving trips around Britain, Ireland, Norway and other sites in northwest Europe. A large number of friends, colleagues and nudibranch enthusiasts have provided support and some of them have also been generous in allowing the use of their photos: Jim Anderson, Jon Chamberlain, Hayden Close, Pierre Corbrion, Charlotte Cumming, Roy Dahl, Sue Daly, Ariane Dimitris, David Fenwick, Giulia Furfaro, Terry Griffiths, Viktor Grøtan, Nicolas Joault, Mats Larsson, Paula Lightfoot, Michael Lundin, Enric Madrenas, Klas Malmgren, Tamsyn Mann, Manon Marco, David Martinez, Allen Murray, Fredrik Pleijel, Miquel Pontes, Poul Eric Rasmussen, Chris Rickard, François Roche, Xavier Rufray, Hazel Selley, J. P. Silva, Christian Skauge, Erling Svensen, Rudolph Svensen, Egidio Trainito, Steve Trewhella and Michiel Vos.

Irish Nudibranch Surveys These have been held at Strangford Lough with support from Queen's University Marine Laboratory in Portaferry (Julia Sigwart); Connemara at Scubadive West (Breffni and Cillian Gray), and Rathlin Island and Portrush with Aquaholics Dive Centre (Richard Lafferty). A great team of nudibranch enthusiasts took part in these surveys; we would especially like to thank Jim Anderson, George Brown, Erling Svensen, Mats Larsson, Michael Lundin, Fred Pleijel, Lydia White, Jon Chamberlain, Guillem Mas, Irene Figueroa, Becky Hitchin, Ross Bullimore, Donna Conroy, Joe Breen, Sally Stewart-Moore, Iain Dixon, Karin Fletcher, Lilian Schoonderwoerd and Carla van Westing.

Skomer Marine Conservation Zone Nudibranch Diversity Surveys (2002–2022) We would like to thank all of the wonderful team at Skomer MCZ who have been running nudibranch monitoring surveys since 2002; Kate Lock, Phil Newman, Mark Burton, Jen Jones, Ross Bullimore and Blaise Bullimore.

Gulen Nudibranch Safari An annual event held at Gulen Dive Resort, Norway. Special thanks to Ørjan Sandnes, Monica Bakkeli, Christian Skauge, Torkild Bakken, Jussi Evertsen, Guido Schmitz, Jorn Ari, Poul Eric Rasmussen, Fredrik Pleijel, Bjørnar Nygård, Klas Malmberg, Sasha Martynov and Tanya Korshunova.

Marine Conservation Society Seasearch Supported a number of dive trips around the UK, and we would like to thank Claire Goodwin, David Kipling, Sarah Bowen, Sally Stewart-Moore, Joe Breen, Libby Keatley and the many Seasearch divers who have contributed records to the national recording schemes.

We would like to especially acknowledge Tom Thompson, Greg Brown, Elizabeth Platts and David Erwin who were responsible for introducing Bernard to nudibranchs and getting him a job where he could pursue the study of marine life.

Finally we would like to thank Julie Dando at Wild Nature Press for accepting the challenge of getting this book to print and making many suggestions to improve its consistency and accuracy, and Robert Kirk at Princeton University Press.

Introduction

This guide is intended for divers, underwater photographers, naturalists exploring the seashore and anyone who wants to know a little more about the nudibranchs found around the coasts of northwest Europe. It is an updated revision of *A Field Guide to the Nudibranchs of the British Isles* which was published in 1994 and was restricted to the species that had been reported from the coasts of Britain and Ireland. Since 1994 two factors have increased the number of species in this region. Firstly, insights from the application of DNA sequence data in nudibranch taxonomy has resulted in the splitting of what were previously considered single species. Secondly, there has been a substantial increase in the occurrence of more southern species being recorded for the first time from the southwestern coasts of Britain. Several of these are represented by relatively large and flamboyantly coloured nudibranchs, and it is more likely that these represent a recent, northward extension of range rather than previously overlooked species. As our seas warm as a consequence of climate change, it is likely that the trend in more southern species moving northwards will continue.

The guide covers nudibranch species that have been recorded from the northwest coasts of Europe from Brest on the Atlantic coast of France to Bodø in Norway and covers approximately 167 species. We have also briefly covered many of the sea slugs which are not nudibranchs, including sea hares, bubble shells and sacoglossans. It is illustrated with photographs of the animals in situ to aid finding them in the field, and studio photographs showing a close-up of the animal and photographs of the often-distinctive spawn. The text has been kept as untechnical as possible, and glossaries are provided to help with specialised terms and scientific names. All of the nudibranchs known from the region are covered together with a few which do not have names at present. A list of further reading is included for those who wish to delve further into nudibranch biology.

The name nudibranch means 'naked gill'; the name refers to the external respiratory organs, such as the branchial plume of dorid nudibranchs, the club-like or arborescent processes found in the cladobranchs and the gills of some species which are located in a lateral groove. Nudibranchs belong to a class of molluscs called the gastropods, which include whelks, periwinkles and limpets. Terrestrial air breathing snails and slugs are now known to be descended from sea slugs, and the group which was formerly called opisthobranchs is now called Heterobranchia to reflect the merger of Opisthobranchia with Pulmonata. Nudibranchs are heterobranch molluscs in which the adult stage has completely lost both the shell and operculum. The loss of the shell has allowed a diverse array of body forms within this order. Nudibranchia is divided into two suborders: Doridina and Cladobranchia. The technical terms used in this book to describe the main morphological features of nudibranchs are described in the section on anatomy and listed in the glossary.

SPECIES NAMES

Scientific names

While well-known species of plants and vertebrates tend to have vernacular (common) names, most marine invertebrates are rarely encountered and have only scientific names, and this is certainly the case for nudibranchs. Linnaeus (1758), often described as the father of taxonomy, developed a system for the naming and classifying of organisms known as the binomial classification. Every species has a two-part name, e.g., *Doris sticta*. The first part of the name tells us that the species belongs to the genus *Doris*; the second part is specific for that species and is known as the specific epithet. The specific epithet is often descriptive; e.g., *sticta* is from the Greek *stikte* – tattooed or spotted – in this case referring to the spotted appearance of this nudibranch. Within zoology each binomial name is unique for that species.

Vernacular names

Unlike scientific names, vernacular names are not unique, and sometimes this can lead to confusion; e.g., Sea Lemon refers to the common intertidal nudibranch *Archidoris pseudoargus* in Europe, but in the northeast Pacific it is used for *Peltodoris nobilis*. Another disadvantage of vernacular names is that they do not imply relatedness to other species. The scientific name tells us that this species is most closely related to other members of the genus *Archidoris*. As this is a unique name, it is also easy to search for information on this species and its closest relatives. The vernacular name 'sea lemon' tells us nothing about the evolutionary relationships of this species and makes finding information on this species difficult.

Why names change

The naming of animals follows guidance set out by the International Code of Zoological Nomenclature (ICZN) which provides rules governing how animals should be named and how to resolve cases where two or more names have been used for the same species; e.g., *Cuthona nana* (Alder & Hancock, 1842) was described by Alder & Hancock in 1842; subsequently they described *Eolis peachii* Alder & Hancock, 1848. In 1980 Greg Brown argued that *Eolis peachii* was the same species as *Cuthona nana*. The ICZN stipulates that the older name has priority and must replace the more recent name; therefore the accepted name is *Cuthona nana* and *Eolis peachii* becomes a junior synonym. There are several reasons why taxonomists change the names of organisms. As our knowledge increases, new evidence may indicate that a species fits better somewhere else; e.g., some species assigned to *Tritonia* have been transferred to *Duvaucelia*. Names can also change as our knowledge increases; e.g., a detailed study of the widespread and common aeolid nudibranch *Aeolidia papillosa* using a combination of morphology and DNA sequences revealed it was in fact several species. In addition to *A. papillosa*, there is now a second species, *A. filomenae*, which also occurs in northwest Europe.

FOOD AND FEEDING IN NUDIBRANCHS

All known nudibranchs are carnivorous, and most are specialised predators with a very selective choice of prey organisms. Species within a family usually feed on similar types of prey. For some species metamorphosis of the larval stage into the adult has been demonstrated to be triggered by the presence of the particular prey species. The lifespan of a nudibranch may also be linked to that of its prey, and two categories are recognised: Nudibranchs that feed upon ephemeral prey, such as hydroids, tend to exhibit several short-lived generations each year. Those that feed upon unseasonal prey, such as sponges and Dead Man's Fingers, may live for one year or possibly longer.

Nudibranchs feed by means of a specialised structure called a radula. This organ is only found in molluscs. The radula consists of many rows of chitinous teeth secreted by the radula sac. In the sponge-feeding cryptobranch dorids, the radula is generally broad, with many teeth in each row. Phanerobranch dorids have much narrower radulae, usually with a pair of large teeth for cutting open bryozoans or ascidians. Aeolid radulae have a central horseshoe-shaped tooth with a strong central denticle, usually flanked by smaller denticles. In the Coryphellidae, Cumanotidae, Flabellinidae and Eubranchidae there is also a pair of lateral teeth.

The shape and number of radular teeth usually show variation from species to species, and radula morphology is an important character used in nudibranch taxonomy. Descriptions of the radulae, though not provided by this field guide, are adequately covered in Thompson & Brown's 1984 book, *Biology of Opisthobranch Molluscs, Volume 2*.

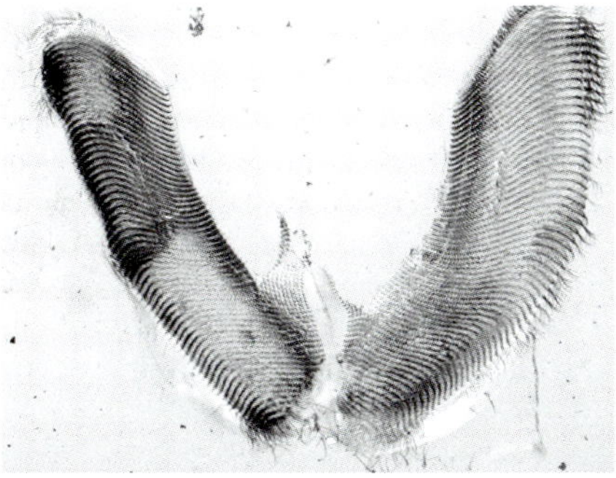

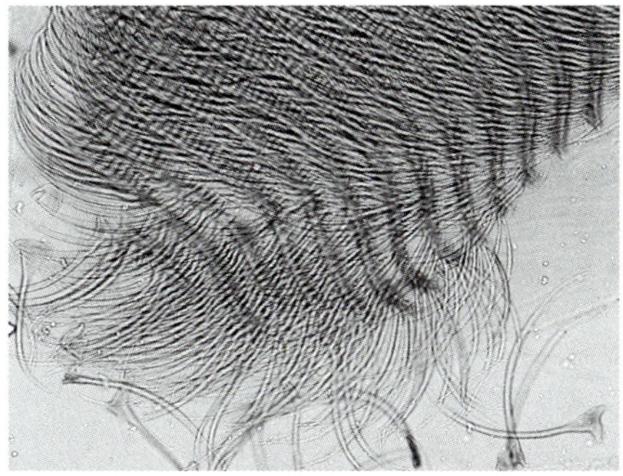

Above left Whole radula of *Rostanga rubra*, a dorid, with 65 rows with 65 teeth per half row and no central tooth (formula 65 x 32.32.1.0.1.32.32).

Above right Detail of radula of *Rostanga rubra* showing spine-like lateral teeth.

Right Radula of *Cumanotus beaumonti*, a cladobranch, showing strong horseshoe-shaped central tooth with main cusp and lateral denticles and one pair of lateral teeth per row (formula 1.1.1).

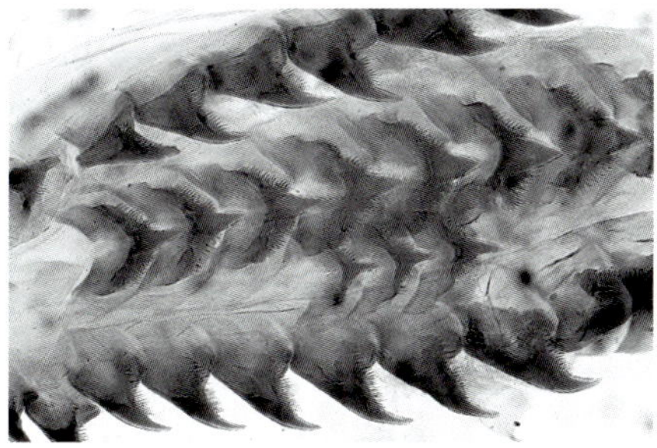

Food preferences of nudibranchs from northwest Europe

Nudibranch species	Food preferences
DORIDINA Dorid nudibranchs all have a rosette of branched gills surrounding the anus in the posterior region of their backs. True dorids such as *Archidoris* have broad radulae with typically 20–60 teeth per row and feed on sponges. Phanerobranch dorids such as *Polycera* and *Onchidoris* have narrow radulae typically with two principal teeth and usually a series of smaller hooks or plates. They feed on bryozoans or tunicates, and a few have odd diets such as *Onchidoris bilamellata*, which eats barnacles.	
Goniodoris castanea	*Botryllus schlosseri*, *Botrylloides leachii*, *Botrylloides diegensis*
Goniodoris nodosa	*Dendrodoa grossularia*, *Alcyonidium* spp.
Lophodoris danielsseni	Ctenostome bryozoans
Okenia aspersa	?*Molgula* spp.
Okenia elegans	*Polycarpa scuba*
Okenia leachii	?*Eugyra arenosa*, *Molgula occulta*
Okenia pulchella	*Molgula occulta*
Ancula cristata	Entoprocts (Kamptozoa) e.g. *Pedicillina* spp.
Trapania maculata	Entoprocts (Kamptozoa) e.g. *Pedicillina* spp.
Trapania pallida	Entoprocts (Kamptozoa) e.g. *Pedicillina* spp.
Trapania tartanella	Entoprocts (Kamptozoa) e.g. *Pedicillina* spp.

Nudibranch species	Food preferences
Acanthodoris pilosa	*Alcyonidium gelatinosum*, ctenostome bryozoans
Adalaria loveni	*Membranipora membranacea*, *Electra pilosa*, *Securiflustra securifrons*
Adalaria proxima	*Electra pilosa*
Onchidoris bilamellata	Barnacles
Atalodoris depressa	*Schizomavella linearis*, *Parasmittina trispinosa*
Atalodoris inconspicua	*Cellepora pumicosa*, *Porella concinna*
Onchidoris muricata	*Membranipora membranacea*, *Securiflustra securifrons*
Atalodoris oblonga	*Cellaria fistulosa*
Atalodoris pictoni	*Reptadeonella violacea*
Atalodoris pusilla	*Escharella immersa*, *Porella concinna*, *Schizomavella linearis*
Atalodoris sparsa	*Cellepora pumicosa*, *Porella concinna*, *Escharoides coccinea*
Diaphorodoris luteocincta	*Nolella* spp.
Corambe testudinaria	*Membranipora membranacea*
Crimora papillata	*Chartella papyracea*, *Flustra foliacea*, *Securiflustra securifrons*
Aegires punctilucens	*Leucosolenia botryoides*, possibly other calcareous sponges
Limacia clavigera	*Electra pilosa*, various encrusting bryozoa
Polycera capitata	*Electra pilosa*, *Membranipora membranacea*
Polycera kernowensis	*Bicellariella ciliata*, branching bryozoans
Polycera quadrilineata	*Membranipora membranacea*
Polycera faeroensis	*Caberea ellisii*, *Crisia* spp., *Bicellariella ciliata*, Bugulidae
Greilada elegans	*Bugula turbinata*
Palio dubia	*Eucratea loricata*
Palio nothus	*Amathia* spp.
Thecacera pennigera	*Bugula plumosa*
Cadlina laevis	*Dysidea fragilis*, *Halisarca dujardini*
Cadlina pellucida	*Spongia lamella*
Felimida krohni	Sponges, Darwinellidae
Aldisa zetlandica	*Hymedesmia* spp.
Rostanga rubra	*Ophlitaspongia papilla*
Thordisa azmanii	*Raspailia ramosa*, *Raspailia hispida*
Doris verrucosa	*Hymeniacidon perleve*, Halichondriidae
Doris cf. *ocelligera*	*Suberites ficus*, Halichondriidae
Doris sticta	*Ciocalypta penicillus*, *Homaxinella subdola*, Halichondrida
Archidoris pseudoargus	*Halichondria panicea*, *Halichondria bowerbanki*, *Hymeniacidon perleve*, *Suberites ficus*
Dendrodoris limbata	Unknown, possibly haplosclerid sponges, *Haliclona* spp.

Nudibranch species	Food preferences
Atagema gibba	*Haliclona fibulata*?
Discodoris rosi	*Clathria* (*Microciona*) *strepsitoxa*
Geitodoris planata	*Mycale rotalis*, *Mycale contarenii*, *Mycale* spp.
Aporodoris millegrana	Unknown
Jorunna tomentosa	*Haliclona* spp.
Jorunna artsdatabankia	*Haliclona urceolus*
CLADOBRANCHIA	
Arminidae have gills in a slit between the mantle edge and foot. They feed on sea pens.	
Armina loveni	*Virgularia mirabilis*
Janolidae have cerata like those of aeolids, but without cnidosacs. They feed on bryozoans.	
Antiopella cristata	*Bugula* spp.
Janolus hyalinus	Candidae spp., *Bugula* spp.
Heroidae have branched cerata like those of tritoniids and dendronotids, but have smooth rhinophores without basal sheaths, like many aeolids. They feed on hydroids.	
Hero formosa	*Tubularia indivisa*
Tritoniidae have branched cerata like those of dendronotids. They feed on soft corals.	
Tritonia hombergii	*Alcyonium digitatum*
Duvaucelia lineata	*Sarcodictyon catenatum*
Duvaucelia manicata	*Cornularia cornucopiae*
Duvaucelia odhneri	*Eunicella verrucosa*
Duvaucelia plebeia	*Alcyonium digitatum*
Lomanotus genei	*Nemertesia* spp.
Lomanotus marmoratus	*Nemertesia antennina*
Scyllaea pelagica	Found amongst the floating gulf weed *Sargassum bacciferum*, feeding on small calyptoblastic hydroids
Hancockia uncinata	*Clytia hemisphaerica*
Dendronotus europaeus	*Tubularia indivisa*
Dendronotus lacteus	*Obelia geniculata*
Dendronotus frondosus	*Sertularia argentea*, other hydroids
Doto coronata	*Sertularia argentea*, *Obelia geniculata*, *Diphasia rosacea*, other hydroids
Doto cuspidata	*Nemertesia ramosa*
Doto dunnei	*Kirchenpaueria pinnata*
Doto eireana	*Amphisbetia operculata*
Doto floridicola	*Aglaophenia kirchenpaueri*
Doto fragilis	*Nemertesia antennina*, *N. ramosa*, *Halecium halecinum*, *H. muricatum*
Doto hydrallmaniae	*Hydrallmania falcata*
Doto hystrix	*Schizotricha frutescens*

Nudibranch species	Food preferences
Doto koenneckeri	*Aglaophenia pluma*
Doto lemchei	*Aglaophenia tubulifera*
Doto maculata	*Halopteris catharina*
Doto millbayana	*Plumularia setacea*
Doto onusta	*Dynamena pumila*
Doto pinnatifida	*Nemertesia antennina*
Doto sarsiae	*Coryne eximia*
Doto tuberculata	*Sertularella gayi*
Embletonia pulchra	?*Halammohydra*
Aeolidioidea and Fionoidea Aeolid nudibranchs are elongate agile molluscs with numerous cerata on their backs. Most feed on various hydroids, with a smaller number in the family Aeolidiidae feeding on sea anemones and a few such as the egg-eating *Favorinus* spp. and *Calma* spp. with more unusual diets. They are the nudibranchs in which the stinging cells from their cnidarian diet are transferred through the digestive gland in the cerata to the terminal cnidosacs, for use in defence of the nudibranch.	
Fjordia browni	*Tubularia indivisa*, *Corymorpha nutans*
Fjordia chriskaugei	*Tubularia indivisa*, other athecate hydroids
Fjordia lineata	*Tubularia indivisa*, *Corymorpha nutans*, *Bougainvillea* spp.
Gulenia borealis	Small athecate hydroids, *Funiculina quadrangularis*
Gulenia monicae	*Eudendrium* spp., small athecate hydroids
Gulenia orjani	*Eudendrium islandicum*, small athecate hydroids
Borealea nobilis	*Ectopleura larynx*, *Athecate hydroids*
Microchlamylla gracilis	*Eudendrium* spp.
Coryphella verrucosa	*Tubularia indivisa*
Coryphella rufibranchialis	Various hydroids, *Tubularia indivisa*
Edmundsella pedata	*Eudendrium ramosa*, other *Eudendrium* spp.
Carronella pellucida	*Eudendrium arbuscula*
Babakina anadoni	the aberrant hydroid *Myriothela cocksi*
Rubramoena amoena	*Halecium halecinum*, *Halecium beanii*
Trinchesia caerulea	*Sertularella polyzonias*, *Sertularella gayi*
Trinchesia cuanensis	*Sertularella polyzonias*, other *Sertularella* spp.
Cuthonella concinna	*Sertularia argentea*
Trinchesia foliata	*Obelia* spp.
Trinchesia genovae	Thecate hydroids
Trinchesia morrowae	*Sertularella* spp., ?*Laomedea angulata*
Cuthona nana	*Hydractinia echinata*
Zelentia pustulata	*Halecium muricatum*

Nudibranch species	Food preferences
Rubramoena rubescens	*Halecium halecinum*
Diaphoreolis viridis	*Sertularella rugosa*, *Sertularella gayi*
Catriona gymnota	*Ectopleura larynx*
Tenellia adspersa	*Cordylophora lacustris*, *Laomedea* spp.
Tergipes tergipes	*Obelia geniculata*, *Laomedea* spp., *Bougainvillea* spp.
Calma glaucoides	Fish eggs, especially clingfish
Calma gobioophaga	Fish eggs, gobies preferred
Fiona pinnata	Goose barnacles, *Velella velella*
Pseudovermis boadeni	*Halammohydra vermiformis*
Amphorina andra	*Obelia* spp., *Laomedea* spp.
Amphorina farrani	*Obelia* spp., *Aglaophenia pluma*
Amphorina linensis	*Laomedea* spp., *Obelia* spp.
Amphorina pallida	*Obelia dichotoma*, *Halecium halecinum*
Capellinia fustifera	*Kirchenpaueria similis*
Eubranchus exiguus	*Obelia geniculata*
Eubranchus tricolor	*Nemertesia ramosa*, *Nemertesia antennina*
Eubranchus vittatus	*Kirchenpaueria pinnata*
Cumanotus beaumonti	*Corymorpha nutans*, Tubulariidae
Xenocratena suecica	Unknown, possibly Edwardsiidae anemones
Facelina annulicornis	Hydroids, other aeolids
Facelina bostoniensis	*Clava multicornis*, *Tubularia indivisa*, *Ectopleura larynx*
Facelina auriculata	*Tubularia indivisa*, *Ectopleura larynx*
Facelina dubia	*Ectopleura larynx*
Caloria elegans	?Athecate hydroids
Favorinus blianus	Nudibranch eggs
Favorinus branchialis	Nudibranch eggs
Pruvotfolia pselliotes	Possibly other nudibranchs, various hydroids
Dicata odhneri	Unknown, small hydroids
Aeolidia papillosa	*Metridium plumosum*
Aeolidia filomenae	*Actinia equina*, *Actinothoe sphyrodeta*, *Anemonia viridis*
Aeolidiella alderi	*Cereus pedunculatus*, *Diadumene cincta*
Aeolidiella cf. *glauca*	*Sagartiogeton laceratus*
Aeolidiella glauca	*Cylista elegans*
Aeolidiella sanguinea	*Sagartia elegans*
Berghia norvegica	*Gonactinia prolifera* anemones
Berghia coerulescens	*Aiptasia couchii*, anemones
Cerberilla bernadettae	?Edwardsiidae anemones

REPRODUCTION IN NUDIBRANCHS

Nudibranchs are simultaneous hermaphrodites; that is, they possess both male and female sex organs and copulation is usually reciprocal, both individuals donating and storing sperm. The reproductive organs open on the right-hand side of the body, and individuals copulate facing in opposite directions with their right sides together. Hermaphrodism has the advantage that any mature individual of the same species encountered is a potential mate, thereby increasing the chances of fertilisation, and each individual can lay eggs, thereby maximising reproductive effort.

Nudibranchs usually lay their spawn on the organism on which they feed, or on a prominent object nearby. Often the spawn is the only indicator that the nudibranchs are present, and it is only on closer inspection that the adult animals are found. The size, shape and colour of nudibranch spawn show great variation from species to species and is a character used in the identification of species.

Development in nudibranchs is usually incomplete; that is, there is a larval stage known as a veliger. The veliger hatches and drifts in the plankton; often the larva will only settle and metamorphose into the adult form in the presence of its particular prey species. In a few species development is completed within the egg and the veliger is not released. This is known as direct development and a minature form of the adult emerges from the egg. In species with planktonic dispersal the eggs are small and take only a short period to hatch. However, in species with direct development the egg size tends to be large since it is essential that it contains sufficient food to nourish the embryo through to the juvenile stage.

Mating pair of *Trapania maculata*. (Enric Madrenas)

Cross species mating: *Fjordia browni* and *F. chriskaugei.*

ANATOMY

The shell

In nudibranch molluscs the shell is only present in the larval stage. The loss of the shell in adults is probably responsible for the diversity of body forms present within this order.

The mantle

In typical dorid nudibranchs, the mantle is thick and extends over the foot. The surface of the mantle may bear tubercles which vary in size, shape and number and are often a character used to identify nudibranchs. In many dorids acid glands and/or spicules are incorporated in the mantle tissue, and it is thought that these are mainly defensive in function. However, in goniodorids, polycerids and some other dorid families the mantle is progressively reduced to a ridge around the side of the body, from which pallial tentacles or processes arise. These processes usually have coloured tips and contain defensive glands and have been shown to produce chemicals distasteful to fish. These chemicals are often manufactured from similar chemical compounds in the bryozoan or ascidian prey or may be the same molecules selectively re-secreted by the nudibranch.

In aeolid nudibranchs the mantle is extended into long finger-like projections called cerata (singular: ceras). The cerata contain branches of digestive gland, and often this is visible through the ceratal epidermis. In aeolids the tips of the cerata contain cnidosacs which usually store nematocysts (stinging cells) that are obtained from ingested cnidarian prey, such as hydroids, sea anemones and soft corals. If disturbed, the nudibranch can discharge these stinging cells through a terminal pore in the ceras; this is an effective deterrent to predatory fish.

The rhinophores

The head region of nudibranchs bears a pair of sensory tentacles called rhinophores. These structures are primarily chemosensory (smell, taste) in function. In many dorid nudibranchs the rhinophores can be retracted into a basal sheath. The shape of the rhinophores varies greatly from one species to another.

The gills

In nudibranchs the gills are probably the most important respiratory organ; however, gaseous exchange also occurs over the entire body surface. In dorids the gills consist of several feather-like structures that encircle the anus. This structure is termed the **branchial plume** and is situated in the posterior part of the animals' back. In true dorids (i.e., Dorididae, Rostangidae, Chromodorididae, etc.) the gills can be retracted into a gill-pocket. These dorids are known as cryptobranch dorids, as opposed to phanerobranch dorids in which the gills are contractile but not retractile into a pocket. Goniodorids, onchidorids and polycerids are phanerobranch dorids. In aeolids the cerata function as gills. The ceratal epidermis is thin enough to enable oxygen from the surrounding water to diffuse in and carbon dioxide (a waste product of respiration) to diffuse out. In the other cladobranchs the cerata are branched or tuberculate, increasing the surface area available for gas exchange. In the Arminidae leaf-like gills are hidden in a groove between the mantle and foot.

The oral veil

In some nudibranchs the front region of the head is extended to form an oral veil. This structure varies from one species to another e.g., in *Dendronotus frondosus* it has branched processes; in *Polycera quadrilineata* it forms up to six finger-like processes and in *Doto* species it is smooth edged with two lateral flaps, called oral lobes.

The oral tentacles

Most nudibranch species have a pair of processes, one on either side of the mouth, which are probably involved in identifying food by taste or touch. The front of the foot may be rounded or extended laterally as a pair of propodial tentacles.

Dorid anatomy

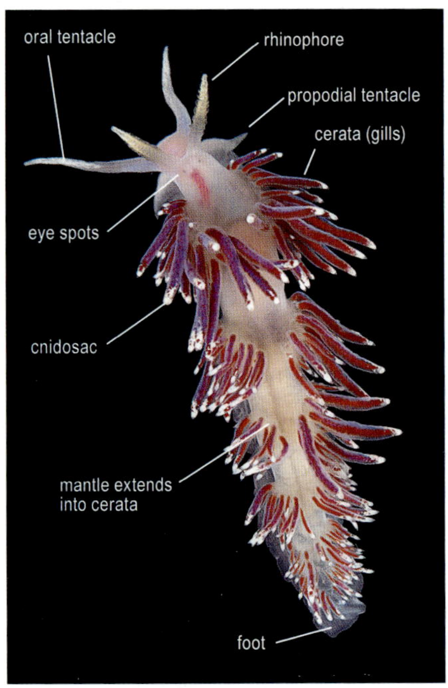

Cladobranch anatomy

FINDING NUDIBRANCHS

Look for spawn. Nudibranchs all lay slightly different shaped egg masses; these are usually white, but may be pink, yellow, or orange. They are usually conspicuous and are laid in prominent places. Search nearby for the animal, which may be beneath a rock or at the base of the hydroids or bryozoans on which the eggs are laid. Try collecting clumps of hydroids with eggs on and leaving these for a few hours in trays of seawater when the animals will probably crawl out or float upside down on the water surface.

Look under rocks and at night. Some aeolids and many dorids are nocturnal, especially in the tropics. They may be easier to find at night, when they come out to lay eggs, or may be found in the daytime by turning over loose rocks, broken corals, etc. Take care to turn any rocks back after searching under them.

Know the likely food of your animals. Sponge feeders will usually stay on their food and move about very little, except to lay eggs. Sponges are commoner in deeper water, in caves, under overhangs and under rocks, in places more or less out of the light. Bryozoan feeders are somewhat more active but are again usually on or amongst their food. Hydroid feeders are quite active and are usually found amongst their food or crawling nearby. Soft coral and coral feeders are often well camouflaged and may eat their way into the food or live near the bases of large colonies. Some nudibranchs feed on burrowing anemones or sea pens and may burrow in gravel, sand, or mud.

Nudibranchs vary in size, from about 5 mm as in the *Goniodoris nodosa* seen here next to a much larger *Fjordia browni,* Gulen, Norway.

RECORDING NUDIBRANCHS

There are a variety of local and national online recording schemes for the different countries within the area covered by this guide. iNaturalist is a global recoding scheme for mapping and sharing biological records and is supported by the California Academy of Sciences and the National Geographic Society. It connects observers with a community of users who can assist with the identification and verification of records. The iNaturalist platform is evidence based and requires the submission of photographs or in the case of animals such as birds, recordings of bird calls. Verified records are shared with the Global Biodiversity Information Facility (GBIF) and in the UK, the National Biodiversity Network (NBN). iNaturalist includes an automated species identification tool in which submitted photos can be identified using computer-based identification software which has been trained using the extensive database of observations on iNaturalist (113,519,482 observations accessed on 03.09.2022).

GLOSSARY

anterior towards the front of the body
arborescent tree-like
athecate gymnoblastic hydroids
bipinnate branched twice
calyptoblastic hydroids with complete thecal cups around the polyps
carnivorous feeds on other animals
chitin a tough membranous protein material
circalittoral the region dominated by sessile animals, found below the algal zone
clavus the stem of the rhinophore if the rhinophore has lamellae or other surface area increasing folds
colonial usually applied to animals in which identical individuals are united together, forming a colony
conulose conical in shape
dorsal the back or upper surface
dorsum the back of the animal
ephemeral seasonal organisms that usually die back in winter
epidermis skin
fucoids brown algae of the family Fucaceae, e.g., bladder wrack
gill respiratory organ
gymnoblastic hydroids in which the polyps are not surrounded by thecal cups
infralittoral the algal dominated zone below low water mark
interstitially living between sand grains
intertidal the region of the shore between high and low tide
lamellate with a series of flattened lateral plates
mantle rim the edge of the mantle; in many nudibranchs this is reduced to a ridge along the sides of the body, from which processes or cerata arise
mucronate a rounded shape, drawn out into a point at the tip
nematocyst stinging cells found in cnidarians
notum the back of a sea slug
operculum a horny plate that seals the opening of the shell; this is absent in adult nudibranchs, but present in the larval stage
ovotestis male and female gonads
pallial rim mantle rim
papillae growths extending from the mantle edge or surface of the body
pedunculate stalked
phanerobranch gills that cannot be retracted into a gill-pocket
posterior the tail end of the animal
prey an animal on which another animal feeds
reticulate a pattern of straight lines or ridges joining at angles
sessile living attached to the substratum
spawn mass of eggs embedded in transparent jelly
spicules rods of calcium carbonate, usually fusiform in shape, supporting the mantle and tubercles in dorids
stellate star-shaped
sublittoral below the low tide level
subterminal just below the end or tip of a process
synonym a newer name given inadvertently to a species already described
taxonomy the classification of organisms into related groups in a hierarchical manner
tentacle a long sensory process
tubercle a rounded swelling, found on the dorsal surface of many dorid nudibranchs
velum a ciliated pair of lobes, used for swimming and feeding by larval molluscs
ventral the oral surface on the underside of the animal

GLOSSARY OF SCIENTIFIC NAMES

Scientific names of animals are used by biologists all over the world to refer to the same species by the same name. Many people find this daunting at first, but most animals do not have vernacular names, so try not to be put off by scientific ones.

Acanthodoris spiny *Doris*
Acteon character from Greek mythology
adspersa scattered, refers to the pigment spots
Aegires from Aegir, a norse god
Aeolidia from Aeolis, the Greek god of the wind
Aeolidiella diminutive of *Aeolidia*
Akera Egyptian god, symbol of the underworld
alba white
alderi, Alderia after Joshua Alder, British nudibranch pioneer
amoena beautiful, pretty
Amphorina from amphora, Greek pottery container with a pointed bottom, refers to the shape of the cerata
anadoni after Dr Emilio Anadón, a professor of zoology at the University of Oviedo
andra Swedish for second, refers to it being a separate species from *Amphorina viriola*
annulicornis ringed horns
Antiopella from Antiope, from Greek mythology, daughter of Aeolis
Aplysia from Greek *aplytos*, unwashed
Archidoris ancient or original *Doris*
Armina German girl's first name
artsdatabankia after the Norwegian Artsdatabank project
Atalodoris from Greek *atalo*, meaning young
atlanticus Atlantic (Ocean)
aurantia, ***aurantiaca*** becoming orange
auriculata diminutive ears
azmanii after Dr J. Azmani, a medical doctor known to Cervera and Garcia Gómez
Babakina after Kikutaro Baba (1905–2001), worked on the nudibranchs of Japan
beaumonti after Walter Ibbotson Beaumont of Plymouth, a Late Victorian naturalist
bellula from Latin *bella*, meaning beautiful
Berghia after Rudolph Bergh, Danish malacologist
bernadettae Jean Tardy named this species in honour of his wife, Bernadette
Berthella after French naturalist Sabin Berthelot (1794–1880)
bifida branched in two
bilamellata two-layered
blianus after Blia Rock, Norway
Bohuslania after Bohuslän on the west coast of Sweden
Borealea boreal
boadeni after Pat Boaden, Director of Portaferry Marine Station, N. Ireland
bostoniensis after Boston, USA
branchialis from *branchia* = gill
browni after Greg Brown, co-author of Thompson & Brown
caerulea sky blue
Calliopaea from Calliope, a Greek muse
Caloria after Prof Luigi Calori (1807–1896), Professor of the Royal Academy of Sciences at Bologna
Capellinia after Prof Giovanni Capellini (1833–1922), Italian paleontologist
capitata from Latin *capitatus*, meaning head-shaped
Carronella after Loch Carron, a Scottish sea loch
castanea chestnut coloured
Catriona Gaelic girl's name meaning pure, clear
Cerberilla from Cerbère in France
chriskaugei after Christian Skauge
cingulatus ringed, banded
clavigera from *clavus* = club and *gero* = to carry
coerulescens blue
Colpodaspis from Greek *kolpos* = fold + *aspis* = shield
concinna neat
coronata crowned
Coryphella little-headed
Crimora heroine of Gaelic mythology
cristata crested
cuanensis refers to Lough Cuan, the Irish name for Strangford Lough
Cumanotus from Greek *kyma* = wave + notum = back
cuspidata cuspidate, with cusps
danielsseni in honour of Daniel Cornelius Danielssen (1815–1894), a Norwegian zoologist and physician, who is best known for his research on leprosy
Dendronotus from Greek, *dendros* = tree + *notus* = back
depressa flattened
Diaphoreolis diaphanous aeolid
Diaphorodoris diaphanous *Doris*
Dicata from Latin, means dedicated to
Discodoris rounded *Doris*
Doris a sea nymph in Greek mythology,

daughter of the sea gods Oceanus and Tethys.
Doto a sea nymph
dubia doubtful
dunnei after Jimmy Dunne, fish biologist at Galway University
Duvaucelia after Alfred Duvaucel (1792–1824), collector for the natural history museum in Paris
Edmundsella after Dr Malcolm Edmunds, nudibranch taxonomist
eireana after Eire, Ireland
elegans elegant
Embletonia after Denis Embleton, a Victorian anatomist at Newcastle University
Eubranchus true gilled
europaeus from Europe
exiguus small, tiny
Facelina after the Roman goddess of hunting, Diana Facelina
faeroensis from Faeroe Islands
farrani after George Philip Farran, late 19th century marine biologist
Favorinus possibly after French philosopher Favorinus de Arles
filomenae after Matilde Filomena López González, grandmother of Marta Pola
Fjordia from fjord
floridicola from Latin *floris* = flower + *cola* = loving, living amongst
Flabellina fan-like
foliata leaf bearing
formosa beautiful
fragilis fragile
frondosus frondose, bushy
fustifera from Latin *fustis* = club-shaped or knobbed stick, refers to the shape of the cerata
Geitodoris from Greek *geitonos* = similar to, refers to a close relationship with *Doris* nudibranchs
genei after Carlo Giuseppe Gene (1800–1847), Italian entomologist
genovae after Genoa, Italy
gibba, ***gibbosa*** humped
glauca, ***glaucoides*** bluish
Glaucus grey-green, sea god, son of Anthedon
Goniodoris angular-shaped *Doris*
gracilis graceful
griegi after James Alexanderssøn Grieg (1861–1936), a Norwegian zoologist
Gulenia after Gulen in Norway
gymnota naked
Hancockia after Albany Hancock, British nudibranch pioneer
Hermaea after Hermes, messenger to the gods in Greek mythology
Hero from Greek *heros* = demi-god
hombergii after Homberg
hyalinus hyaline, colourless and transparent
hystrix porcupine
inconspicua inconspicuous
Janolus from Janus, a two-headed Greek god
Jorunna possibly after Jorunn Bjarnadottir, a character from an Icelandic saga
Kaloplocamus from Greek *kalos* = good, beautiful + *plokamos* = hair tress
kernowensis from Cornwall
koenneckeri after Gerd Koennecker, diving biologist at Galway University
krohni after Augustus Krohn (1803–1891), Russian zoologist
lacteus milky white
laevis smooth
leachii after William Elford Leach, English marine biologist
lemchei after Henning Lemche, Danish nudibranch worker
lignarius from Latin = related to wood, refers to the colour patternation of the shell
Limacia from *Limax*, a land slug
lineata with lines
linensis after La Línea de la Concepción, a village next to Gibraltar
Lomanotus from Greek *loma* = border + *notus* = back
Lophodoris from Greek *lophos* = height, entrenchment + *Doris* = a sea nymph in Greek mythology
loveni after Sven Lovén, Swedish nudibranch biologist
luteocincta yellow ring
maculata spotted
manicata Latin, with sleeves, refers to the rhinophore sheaths
marmoratus marbled
matsmichaeli after Mats Larsson & Michael Lundin, two Swedish divers and nudibranch enthusiasts
Microchlamylla refers to the vas deferens
millbayana after Millbay, Plymouth, England
modesta modest
monicae after Monica Bakkeli from Gulen Dive Centre
morrowae after Christine Morrow, sponge taxonomist and nudibranch enthusiast
mucroniferus bearing mucros, points
muricata sharp pointed

nana dwarf
navicula small boat
nobilis noble
nodosa bumpy, with nodules
norvegica from Norway
nothus false, mongrel, hybrid
oblonga oblong
ocelligera from Latin *ocellus* = little eye + *gerere* = to bear or carry
odhneri after Nils Odhner, nudibranch biologist
Okenia after Oken, student of Linnaeus
Onchidoris tuberculate *Doris*
onusta full, overloaded
orjani after Ørjan Sandnes from the Gulen Dive Centre
Palio from Latin *pallium* = cloak or coverlet
pallida, ***pallidus*** pale
papillata, ***papillosa*** with papillae, i.e., short processes
pedata refers to the cerata, they are joined at their base, hand-like
pelagica pelagic, floating
pellucida pellucid, transparent
pennigera feather-bearing
Philine from Greek *philaino* = name of two brothers from Greek mythology
pictoni after Bernard Picton, nudibranch taxonomist
pilosa hairy
pinnata pinnate, with opposite pairs of cerata
pinnatifida refers to the arrangement of the cerata, *pinnate* (feather-like), *fidus* (divided)
planata flat
plebeia common, small
Pleurobranchus from Greek *pleuron* = side + *branchus* = gill
plumula plumosa, feathery
Polycera many horns
Proctonotus from Greek *proctus* = anus + *notus* = back
proxima near, close
pruinosa from Latin = frosty
Pruvotfolia after Alice Pruvot-Fol (1873–1972), nudibranch taxonomist
pselliotes from Greek *psellion* = bracelet
pseudoargus false *Argus* (*Doto argus*)
Pseudovermis false worm
pulchra pulchella, pretty
punctata with points
punctilucens points of light
pusilla very small
pustulata pustulose
quadrilineata four-lined
quadripartita from Latin *quadratus* = four + *partitus* = divided
robustus robust
rosi after Joandomenec Ros, opisthobranch expert
Rostanga possibly after Röstånga in Sweden
rubescens reddish, becoming red
rubra red
Rubramoena from *rubra* = red + *amoena* = pretty
rufibranchialis refers to the red cerata
rupium Latin *rupi* = to break
sanguinea blood-red
sarsiae after the hydroid *Sarsia eximia* (now *Coryne eximia*)
Scaphander from Greek *skaphe* = boat or an excavated object + *andros* = man
Scyllaea sea goddess, daughter of Nereis
sparsa sparse
sticta spotted
suecica Swedish
tartanella a type of fishing practised in Italy
Tenellia delicate
testudinaria tortoise shell
Thecacera sheathed processes
Thordisa woman's name, from Norse mythology
tomentosa tomentose, velvety
tornatilis Latin, made on a lathe or rolled, refers to the shell
Trapania the original name of this genus was *Drepania* = sickle-shaped and refers to the accessory appendages to the gills and rhionophores. As *Drepania* was already occupied for a genus of Lepidoptera, the name was changed to *Trapania*
tricolor three coloured
Trinchesia after Salvatore Trinchese (1836–1897), Italian malacologist
Tritonia after Triton, Roman god of the sea
tuberculata tuberculate
uncinata hooked
verrucosa with verrucae
villosa covered with soft hairs
viridis green
viriola from Latin for pustules or pox
vittatus longitudinally striped, banded
Xenocratena from Latin *xeno* = combining form + *cratena*, a genus of aeolid nudibranchs
yrjargul Yrjar is the old name for Ørland in Norway + gul is Norwegian for yellow
Zelentia after Dalnie Zelentsy in the Barents Sea
zetlandica from Shetland

Acanthodoris pilosa (Abildgaard, 1789)

DESCRIPTION *Acanthodoris pilosa* is easily distinguished from other British nudibranchs by its overall 'fluffy' appearance, caused by the presence of long, soft papillae all over the back of the animal. The rhinophores are long, with long shafts below the lamellate portions; the gills are large and fluffy. Colour is variable from white through brown and purple to black. Mature specimens of *A. pilosa* are usually 30 mm in length but may reach almost 70 mm.

ECOLOGY The prey of *A. pilosa* consists of encrusting ctenostome bryozoans such as *Alcyonidium hirsutum* and *Flustrellidra hispida* on shore and the erect fleshy bryozoan *Alcyonidium diaphanum* in the sublittoral.

DISTRIBUTION Common around Britain and Ireland and from Norway to the Mediterranean.

SIMILAR SPECIES The large rhinophores and the long, soft papillae distinguish this species from any other British nudibranch.

KEY CHARACTERISTICS Rounded body with long soft papillae all over. Large rhinophores and gills.

Two individuals on the bryozoan *Alcyonidium diaphanum*, Portrush, Northern Ireland.

Studio shot of adult, Gulen, Norway.

Spawn coil on the bryozoan *Alcyonidium diaphanum*, Cornwall, England.

Adalaria loveni

(Alder & Hancock, 1862)

DESCRIPTION The body of *Adalaria loveni* may be white or yellow in colour, slightly translucent. The mantle is densely covered by large rounded tubercles which are interspersed with smaller tubercles. The rhinophores are lamellate. Up to 32 mm in length.

ECOLOGY Kelp forests in shallow water, feeding on *Membranipora membranacea* and *Electra pilosa*.

DISTRIBUTION The original description gives the locality of the type specimen as Bantry Bay, southwest Ireland, but this may be a mix-up of the original material by Alder & Hancock as specimens have not since been found this far south. Currently this species is found in western Scotland north to Norway and Sweden. Alder & Hancock discuss material from Norway received from Lovén and name the animal after him.

SIMILAR SPECIES Similar in appearance to *Adalaria proxima* (p. 24) but with fewer, larger, flattened tubercles.

KEY CHARACTERISTICS Typical onchidorid shape. Large, flattened tubercles of irregular size.

Two individuals mating on kelp frond with the bryozoan *Membranipora membranacea*, Gulen, Norway.

Studio shot of adult, Gulen, Norway.

Ribbon of spawn on kelp frond, Gulen, Norway.

Adalaria proxima (Alder & Hancock, 1854)

DESCRIPTION The body may be white or yellow in colour. The mantle is covered by rounded tubercles with conical tips. The rhinophores are lamellate, usually they are darker in appearance than the rest of the mantle. The largest specimen recorded was 17 mm. The spawn consists of a spiral ribbon of eggs.

ECOLOGY Usually found feeding on *Electra pilosa*, but reported to eat a variety of encrusting bryozoans. This animal is common on the low shore and in the shallow subtidal amongst bryozoan encrusted seaweeds. Adults may be found spawning on fucoids from February to May.

DISTRIBUTION A northern species in Britain and Ireland, with a single doubtful record from Plymouth. Frequent in the Menai Straits, Strangford Lough and on Scottish coasts. It is found in Norway but records may be confused with *Adalaria loveni*.

SIMILAR SPECIES This species has often been confused with *Onchidoris muricata* (p. 40); however the rhinophores of *Adalaria proxima* are blunter than those of *O. muricata* and the tubercles have pointed rather than flat tops. *Adalaria loveni* (p. 22) is much larger and has fewer tubercles which are very irregular in size.

KEY CHARACTERISTICS White or pale yellow animal with rounded tubercles. Tubercles with pointed tops.

One individual on the bryozoan *Electra pilosa* growing on the brown seaweed *Fucus vesiculosus*, Strangford Lough, Northern Ireland.

Studio shot of adult, Strangford Lough, Northern Ireland.

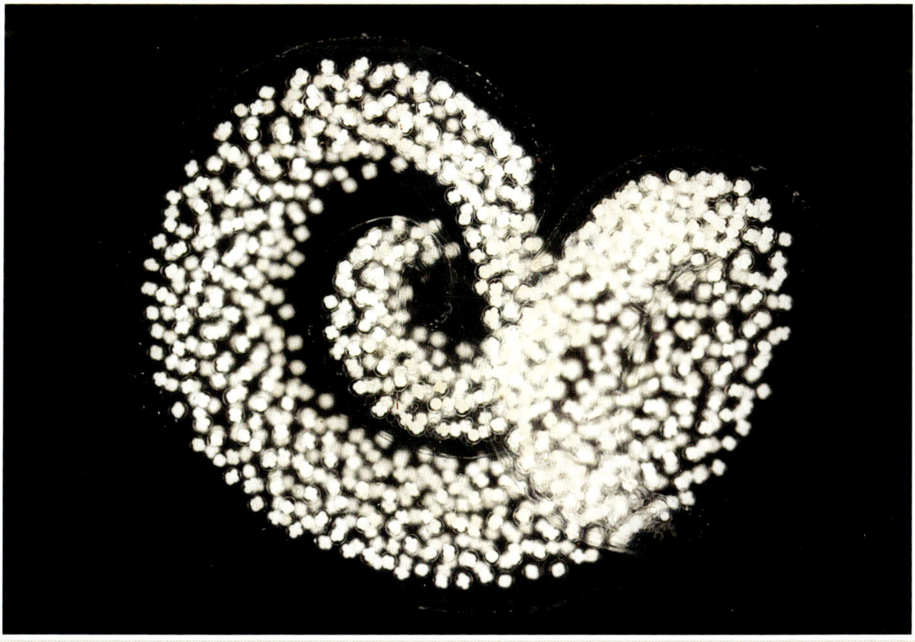

Studio shot of spawn, each egg has four developing larvae, Strangford Lough, Northern Ireland.

Idaliadoris depressa (Alder & Hancock, 1842)

All species of *Idaliadoris* and *Atalodoris* were previously included in the genus *Onchidoris*.

DESCRIPTION *Idaliadoris depressa* is a small, flattened nudibranch, reaching only 9 mm in length. The body is translucent white with regular spots of red-brown pigment that is concentrated on the middle of the back. The spicules that are incorporated in the mantle can be distinguished with a hand lens. This species has distinctive long hairy transparent tubercles all over its back. The rhinophores are lamellate. The spawn is a very fine orange or pink thread laid in a neat spiral.

ECOLOGY This animal feeds on the encrusting bryozoans *Schizomavella linearis* and *Parasmittina trispinosa*. It is often found under stones on the shore or in shallow water, but also on exposed rock faces where *P. trispinosa* is common.

DISTRIBUTION Found around Britain and Ireland, but rarely recorded due to its small size and good camouflage. It has been recorded as far north as Norway and south to the Atlantic coast of France and the Mediterranean Sea.

SIMILAR SPECIES *Idaliadoris neapolitana* and *Idaliadoris cervinoi* (both from Spain and not included here) are very similar (Furfaro *et al.* 2022). *Atalodoris* species (pp. 28–36) all have rounded, short tubercles.

KEY CHARACTERISTICS Long hair-like tubercles and spots of brown pigment. Conspicuous mantle spicules. Flattened body.

One individual, extremely well camouflaged on the bryozoan *Parasmittina trispinosa*, Portaferry, Ireland.

Studio shot of adult, Strangford Lough, Northern Ireland.

Two spawn spirals in an area of the bryozoan *Parasmittina trispinosa* that has been grazed by the adults, Isle of Man.

Atalodoris inconspicua (Alder & Hancock, 1851)

All species of *Idaliadoris* and *Atalodoris* were previously included in the genus *Onchidoris.*

DESCRIPTION This rare animal is white or pale brown in colour and is often tinged with a purple hue. Numerous small specks of brown pigment cover the mantle. The mantle bears many small, rounded tubercles. The rhinophores have about 14 close-set lamellae and there are 10 gills. The largest specimen recorded was 12 mm in length. The spawn is a neatly coiled thin string of eggs, very similar to *Atalodoris sparsa* (p. 37).

ECOLOGY Alder & Hancock collected the original two specimens on the bryozoan *Cellepora pumicosa* 'from the deep-water fishing boats'. *Atalodoris inconspicua* was subsequently reported as feeding on *Cellaria sinuosa*, but this is probably a misidentification of *Atalodoris oblonga*. It has also been found on the bryozoan *Porella concinna*.

DISTRIBUTION Records of this species are few, originally from off Northumberland and more recently from Robin Hood's Bay in the North Sea, Orkney and southern Norway.

SIMILAR SPECIES *Atalodoris sparsa* (p. 36) also feeds on *Cellepora pumicosa* and is similar in colour. However, it can be distinguished by having only 8 or 9 rather distant lamellae on the rhinophores and a conspicuous pattern of larger tubercles around the bases of the rhinophores.

KEY CHARACTERISTICS White animal with irregular spots of purple, brown and yellow. Tubercles with rounded tops. Fourteen closely spaced lamellae on the rhinophores.

Adult on silty bedrock, Egersund, Norway. (Erling Svensen)

Left to right: rhinophores of *Atalodoris inconspicua*, *A. sparsa* and *A. pusilla* (based on Alder & Hancock, 1845–55).

Spawn coil is similar to *A. sparsa* and associated with the above bryozoan *Cellepora pumicosa*.

Atalodoris oblonga (Alder & Hancock, 1845)

All species of *Idaliadoris* and *Atalodoris* were previously included in the genus *Onchidoris*.

DESCRIPTION The body of this nudibranch is narrow in comparison with other onchidorids. The mantle bears small, rounded tubercles and is grey in colour with a few darker blotches on the back. It may grow to 12 mm in length, but most individuals are approximately 5–8 mm long. The spawn consists of a rounded mass of eggs looking like a swelling on the branch of *Cellaria fistulosa*.

ECOLOGY This species is well camouflaged on its prey, *Cellaria fistulosa*, an erect, sublittoral bryozoan.

DISTRIBUTION *Atalodoris oblonga* is found at scattered localities on the southern and western coasts of Britain and Ireland but is rarely recorded. Recent records include Skomer Island, Lundy, Plymouth, the Irish Sea and the west coast of Scotland. Present in southern Norway.

SIMILAR SPECIES The body shape of this species is quite distinctive. It is not flattened as much as other *Atalodoris* species (pp. 28–36) which live on flat bryozoan crusts and keep a low profile.

KEY CHARACTERISTICS Body elongate and rounded in the back, not flattened. Grey-white in colour with slight brown mottling.

Adult on the bryozoan *Cellaria fistulosa*, The Maidens, Northern Ireland.

Studio shot of adult, Skomer, Wales.

Adults and spawn on the bryozoan *Cellaria fistulosa*, The Maidens, Northern Ireland.

Atalodoris pictoni

Furfaro & Trainito, 2017

All species of *Idaliadoris* and *Atalodoris* were previously included in the genus *Onchidoris.*

DESCRIPTION The body is very flattened and rounded and ranges from 9 to 12 mm in length. The mantle is a uniform dark brown with bluish white speckling. The retractable rhinophores have 9 or 10 lamellae, they are long and slender and completely white. The gills consist of 9 or 10 bipinnate branchial leaves that encircle the anus. The underside of the body is light grey with scattered darker speckling. The spawn is a white thread laid in a coil like a watch spring.

ECOLOGY Feeds on the encrusting bryozoan *Reptadeonella violacea*. It has been found on vertical or overhanging rock faces in areas of strong water movement or offshore exposed sites.

DISTRIBUTION The distribution of this recently described species is poorly known. So far it has been recorded from Spain to Sardinia in the Mediterranean Sea, Trieste in the Adriatic Sea and the west coasts of Scotland and Ireland.

SIMILAR SPECIES Previously identified in the Mediterranean as *Atalodoris pusilla* (p. 34), it differs in having brown, not white/translucent, gills (Furfaro & Trainito, 2017).

KEY CHARACTERISTICS Rounded, flattened body with uniform dark brown coloration. Transparent rhinophores and dark brown gills.

Three individuals feeding on the bryozoan *Reptadeonella violacea*, Mayo, Ireland.

Large individual on bryozoan food, Mediterranean coast of Spain. (Enric Madrenas)

Two adults and two spirals of spawn on the bryozoan *Reptadeonella violacea*, Connemara, Ireland.

Atalodoris pusilla (Alder & Hancock, 1845)

All species of *Idaliadoris* and *Atalodoris* were previously included in the genus *Onchidoris*.

DESCRIPTION This animal may reach 9 mm in length. The mantle is pigmented with dark brown pigment spots which may be well spaced or almost coalescing in darker individuals. There are 3 diffuse dark blotches beneath the skin. The tubercles that cover the dorsal surface are very tiny and conical in shape. The rhinophores have 9 rather distant lamellae and both gills and rhinophores are translucent white.

ECOLOGY *Atalodoris pusilla* feeds on a variety of encrusting bryozoans such as *Escharella immersa*, *Porella concinna* and *Schizomavella linearis*. It has been found beneath stones or rocks in areas of strong water movement both intertidally and in shallow water.

DISTRIBUTION Found around the coasts of Britain and Ireland, but rarely recorded. Further distribution includes the French and Spanish Atlantic coasts and Norway.

SIMILAR SPECIES *Atalodoris pictoni* (p. 32) was mistaken for this species in the Mediterranean Sea, but has brown gills and continuous black pigment on the mantle.

KEY CHARACTERISTICS Flattened oval body with sparse to dense, brown or black pigment spots. Transparent gills and rhinophores.

Two adults, Egersund, Norway. (Erling Svensen)

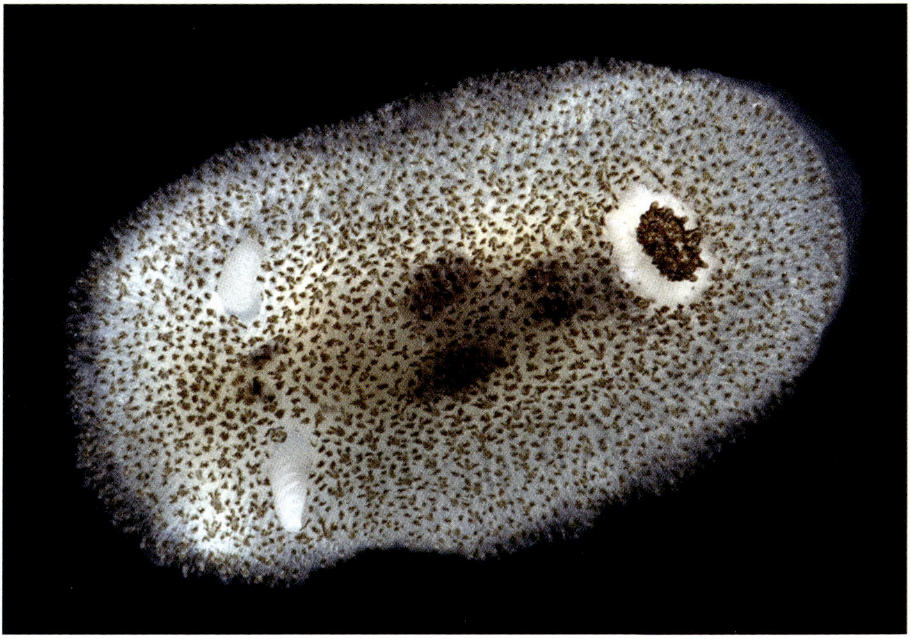

Studio shot of adult, Skomer, Wales.

Adult and spiral of spawn on encrusting bryozoan, Skomer, Wales.

Atalodoris sparsa (Alder & Hancock, 1846)

All species of *Idaliadoris* and *Atalodoris* were previously included in the genus *Onchidoris.*

DESCRIPTION This is a small inconspicuous onchidorid, with a maximum recorded body length of 8 mm, but more usually this nudibranch only grows to 5 mm. *Atalodoris sparsa* has a pale brown mantle with regularly spaced, darker blotches, which may join up into patches. The mantle bears numerous, small, rounded tubercles and there are 3 large tubercles at the base of the rhinophores. The gills form a horseshoe shape around the anus.

ECOLOGY This species feeds on the bryozoans *Cellepora pumicosa* and *Porella concinna* and has been found both on shore and in the sublittoral.

DISTRIBUTION *A. sparsa* is possibly commoner on the northern coasts of Britain and Ireland although there are records from Skomer Island, Plymouth, and the north coast of Spain. As with several other onchidorids it is rarely recorded. It is more frequent in Norway.

SIMILAR SPECIES Careful comparison of the descriptions are necessary to distinguish this species from *Atalodoris inconspicua* (p. 28) and *Idaliadoris depressa* (p. 26).

KEY CHARACTERISTICS Eight or nine rather distant lamellae on the tapering rhinophores. A conspicuous pattern of larger tubercles around the bases of the rhinophores.

Adult feeding on a bryozoan, Gulen, Norway.

Studio shot of adult, Gulen, Norway.

Adult and spawn coil, Egersund, Norway. (Erling Svensen)

Onchidoris bilamellata (Linnaeus, 1767)

DESCRIPTION This nudibranch is usually white with a brown pattern on the mantle; however immature specimens and occasional adults may be all white. The mantle bears many club-shaped papillae. The rhinophores are lamellate and the numerous gills are arranged in a horseshoe. Adults may attain a length of 40 mm. The spawn is a short flat ribbon laid in a curve or concertina shape.

ECOLOGY This species is gregarious, and large numbers of individuals are often found feeding on barnacles on the low shore and sublittorally.

DISTRIBUTION Found around Britain and Ireland and northwards into the Arctic Circle. It reaches the southern limit of its distribution on the French Atlantic coast.

SIMILAR SPECIES *Onchidoris bilamellata* is reported from the Pacific coast of the USA but DNA results indicate that this is a distinct species.

KEY CHARACTERISTICS Grey animal with a brown pigment pattern and rounded tubercles. Numerous (up to 29) retractile gills in a horseshoe.

Three individuals feeding on barnacles, Strangford Lough, Northern Ireland.

Studio shot of adult, Strangford Lough, Northern Ireland.

A congregation of several individuals spawning, Strangford Lough, Northern Ireland.

Onchidoris muricata (O F Müller, 1776)

DESCRIPTION The body may be white or yellow and some rare individuals may have brown speckling on the mantle. The mantle bears flattened, stalked tubercles. The maximum body length is 14 mm. The spawn consists of a ribbon, coiled several times.

ECOLOGY This species feeds on a wide variety of encrusting bryozoans, but it is most often found on *Membranipora membranacea* on the lower shore or on *Securiflustra securifrons* in the sublittoral.

DISTRIBUTION More common in the north of Britain and Ireland than in the south. The species range extends into the Arctic Circle. A few records exist for the French coast.

SIMILAR SPECIES This species is most likely to be confused with *Adalaria proxima* (p. 24), and often they occur together. *Onchidoris muricata* is generally smaller (up to 14 mm), while *A. proxima* can reach 17 mm in length and has tubercles with pointed tops. The radulae are so different that these species are placed in separate genera. White is quite a common colour for dorid nudibranchs and externally *Aldisa zetlandica* (p. 98) juveniles look quite like this species.

KEY CHARACTERISTICS White or yellow animal with rounded tubercles. Tubercles with flattened tops.

Two individuals on the bryozoan *Securiflustra securifrons*, Rathlin Island, Northern Ireland.

Studio shot of adult, Rathlin Island, Northern Ireland.

Several spawn coils on kelp blade with the bryozoan *Electra pilosa*, Gulen, Norway.

Diaphorodoris luteocincta (M Sars, 1870)

DESCRIPTION This animal may grow to up to 11 mm in length. Unlike the species in the family Onchidorididae, *Diaphorodoris luteocincta* has a conspicuous coloration. The mantle is translucent white with conical tubercles and appears mottled due to subsurface spicules. Between the tubercles there is a variable amount of red pigmentation in the centre of the back extending to a yellow submarginal band. This yellow band is irregular and often broken, set in from the edge of the mantle.

ECOLOGY Feeds on the ctenostome bryozoan *Nolella* and is often found on silt-covered rocks or amongst erect bryozoans on vertical rock faces.

DISTRIBUTION Found around Britain and Ireland and reported from Norway to the Mediterranean.

SIMILAR SPECIES Previously confused with *Diaphorodoris alba* (p. 44), which differs in having a continuous band of yellow at the very edge of the mantle.

KEY CHARACTERISTICS White mantle with irregular yellow submarginal rim. Red patch in the centre of the back.

Adult feeding on the bryozoan *Nolella* sp., Skomer, Wales.

Studio shot of adult, Strangford Lough, Northern Ireland.

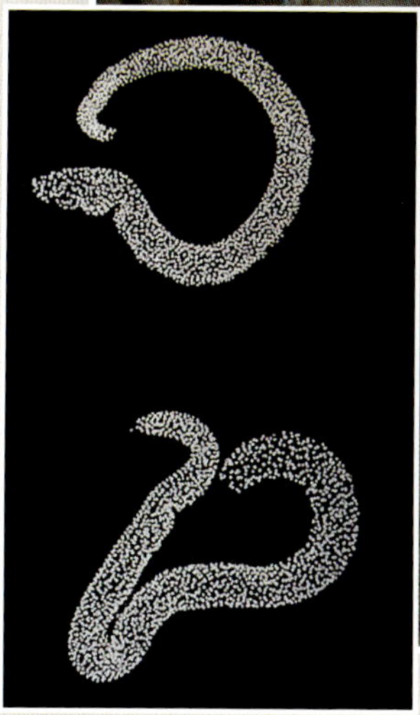

Studio shot of spawn coil, Strangford Lough, Northern Ireland.

Close-up of *Diaphorodoris luteocincta* showing broken, submarginal yellow band. Isle of Man.

Diaphorodoris alba Portmann & Sandmeier, 1960

DESCRIPTION *Diaphorodoris alba* was considered a colour morph of *Diaphorodoris luteocincta* until a recent study by Furfaro *et al.* (2016), using both morphology and DNA, supported the hypothesis that they are distinct species. *D. alba* is usually around 12 mm in length, the body, rhinophore and gills are all white in colour. There is a broad, continuous, yellow ring at the edge of the mantle margin. The mantle is covered in white tubercles that are conical in shape.

ECOLOGY Feeds on the ctenostome bryozoan *Nolella* and can be found with *D. luteocincta* amongst bryozoans on silty rock.

DISTRIBUTION Mediterranean Sea, Atlantic coasts of Europe, southwest England, Wales, northwest Ireland.

SIMILAR SPECIES *D. alba* is similar to *D. luteocincta* (p. 42) but usually lacks the red pigment on the mantle, although some animals have a small amount of red in the centre of the back. In *D. luteocincta* the yellow ring is broken in places and does not extend to the edge of the mantle, whereas in *D. alba* it is unbroken and extends to the mantle edge (Furfaro *et al.*, 2016b).

KEY CHARACTERISTICS White body with yellow marginal ring that extends to the mantle edge.

Adult on bedrock with encrusting bryozoans and coralline algae, Skomer, Wales.

Studio shot of adult, Skomer, Wales.

Diaphorodoris luteocincta, left, meets *D. alba*, right. Martin's Haven, Pembrokeshire, Wales.

Corambe testudinaria

H. Fischer, 1889

DESCRIPTION This species has a body shape similar to *Atalodoris* but there is no gill rosette on the back, just a rim made from a break in the notum surrounding the dorsal anus. The gills are 7–10 leaves in the space between the mantle and the foot, hidden by the mantle. The rhinophores have an incomplete sheath around them, open at the back. The colour pattern is distinctive, consisting of a reticulate pattern of yellow within the transparent mantle, resembling a bryozoan. There are spots in each reticulation, resembling the openings of the bryozoan. It grows to 7 mm in length.

ECOLOGY Feeds on bryozoans. Reported to feed on several bryozoans including *Conopeum reticulatum* and *Electra pilosa*.

DISTRIBUTION Originally described from the French Atlantic coast, this species has been recently found in southwest England. Reported from the French, Spanish and Portuguese Atlantic coasts.

SIMILAR SPECIES The reticulate yellow pattern and pallial gills make this species very distinctive.

KEY CHARACTERISTICS Thin, flat dorid-shaped body with no gill cluster on the back.

Under boulder, Cornwall, England. (Charlotte Cumming)

Under boulder, Cornwall, England. (Charlotte Cumming)

Animal on *Electra pilosa* with spawn coils, Portugal. (J. P. Silva)

Ancula cristata (Alder, 1841)

DESCRIPTION The body of this nudibranch is translucent white. There are up to 7 orange-tipped processes on each side of the gills. A pair of pointed processes project forwards from the base of each rhinophore. White ovotestis is visible through the transparent epidermis. The oral tentacles are short and tipped with orange. Orange pigment is also found on the tips of the rhinophores and on the tip of the tail. Individuals can be found in which the orange pigment is replaced with opaque white. Adult specimens may reach a length of 20 mm.

ECOLOGY This species feeds on minute kamptozoans (Entoprocta) such as *Pedicellina cernua* which are usually epizooic on bryozoa, hydroids, sponges and tunicates, but may also grow on inert surfaces.

DISTRIBUTION *Ancula cristata* is a widely distributed species found from Brittany to Norway. It is found around Britain and Ireland but usually in small numbers. It is apparently rare and confined to cold water in the Mediterranean Sea, and the conspecificity with *Ancula gibbosa* of Risso, 1818 is doubtful.

SIMILAR SPECIES There are several other unrelated species with similar coloration including *Polycera quadrilineata* (p. 90), *Polycera faeroensis* (p. 86), *Polycera kernowensis* (p. 88), *Trapania tartanella* (p. 68) and *Trapania maculata* (p. 64).

KEY CHARACTERISTICS Two anteriorly directed processes at the base of each rhinophore. Several processes at the sides of the gill cluster.

Adult on the bryozoan *Cellaria fistulosa*, Skomer, Wales.

Studio shot of adult, Strangford Lough, Northern Ireland.

Adult and spawn on the hydroid *Sertularella*, Plymouth, England.

Goniodoris castanea

Alder & Hancock, 1845

DESCRIPTION The body of this nudibranch is red-brown in colour and the dorsum is covered with white flecks. There are small ridges and tubercles on the dorsum and flanks. A conspicuous rim runs down the middle of the back and around the edge of the mantle. The rhinophores are lamellate and the small oral tentacles are flattened. This animal may reach 38 mm in length.

ECOLOGY This species feeds on the compound ascidians *Botryllus schlosseri and Botrylloides leachii* and has also been reported as deeply burrowed in the test of *Ascidia mentula*. In the Netherlands it has become common, feeding on the invasive sea squirts *Botrylloides violaceus* and *Botrylloides diegensis* and a wide range of colour forms are present, from orange to white individuals.

DISTRIBUTION Usually found at depths of less than 25 m and sometimes found on the lower shore. Found around Britain and Ireland but occurrence sporadic. Recorded from southern Norway south to the Canary Islands and the western Mediterranean Sea.

SIMILAR SPECIES This species is not easily confused with any others in the northeast Atlantic.

KEY CHARACTERISTICS Thick-set body with ridge at mantle edge and down centre of tail. Front of head with thin mantle ridge with oral tentacles projecting below this.

Underside of boulder on the low shore, County Down, Northern Ireland.

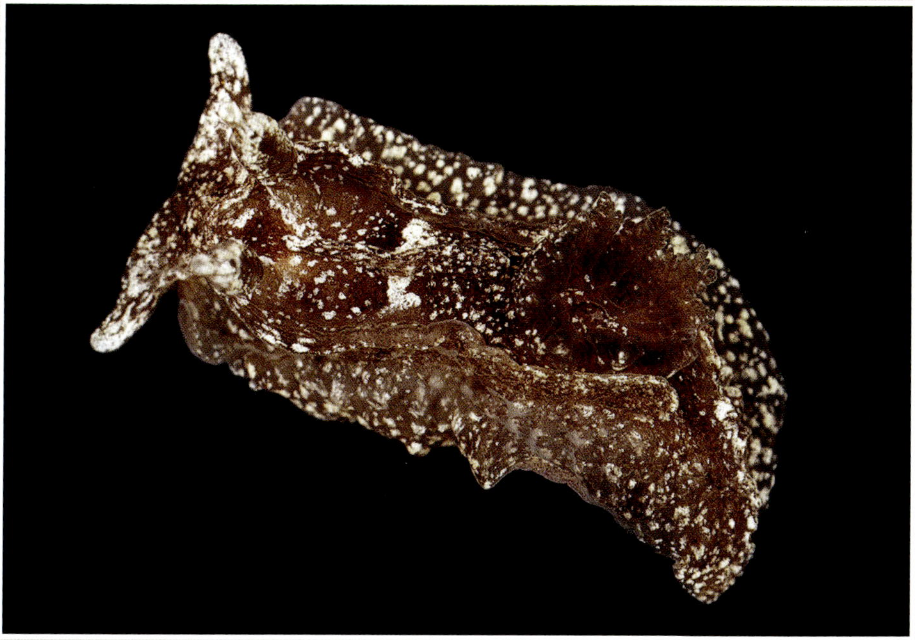

Studio shot of adult, St John's Point, Northern Ireland.

Spawn coil on underside of boulder on the low shore, County Down, Northern Ireland.

Goniodoris nodosa (Montagu, 1808)

DESCRIPTION A translucent white nudibranch with small tubercles and specks of white and/or yellow pigment on its dorsum. An opaque pale yellow ridge runs down the middle of the back to the tip of the tail. There is a transparent patch that is situated just behind the branchial plume, this looks like a small pore on the animal's back. The lamellate rhinophores have a yellow tinge, the oral tentacles are dorso-ventrally flattened. This species may reach a length of 27 mm.

ECOLOGY Juveniles feed on bryozoans, especially *Alcyonidium diaphanum*, but the adults feed on ascidians, especially *Diplosoma listerianum* and *Dendrodoa grossularia*.

DISTRIBUTION Distributed from northwest Spain to the Faeroes and Norway. A common species around Britain and Ireland both on shore and in the shallow sublittoral, it has been recorded at depths down to 120 m.

SIMILAR SPECIES In Norway and the Netherlands *Goniodoris castanea* (p. 50) is sometimes mostly white but differs in having a pronounced rim at the edge of the mantle.

KEY CHARACTERISTICS White animal with reduced thin frilly mantle rim and tail extending at rear. Front of head with oral tentacles visible from above.

Adult on coralline encrusted bedrock, Gulen, Norway.

Studio shot of adult, Skomer, Wales.

Ribbon of spawn on the bryozoan *Alcyonidium diaphanum*, Skomer, Wales.

Lophodoris danielsseni (Friele & Hansen, 1876)

DESCRIPTION The body of this nudibranch is translucent white in colour. The mantle edge is extended and supported by bundles of internal calcareous spicules which terminate in points at the edge. This mantle edge is continuous across the front of the head and broken behind the gills. The last pair of spicule bundles, behind the gill, support a thicker mantle extension which contains yellow glands, and similar glands are at the tip of each gill pinna. There is a jagged keel along the centre of the back, from in front of the rhinophores to the gill cluster. A similar keel runs along the tail. The rhinophores are lamellate. *Lophodoris danielsseni* typically grows to a length of 12 mm. The spawn is unknown.

ECOLOGY This animal feeds on a creeping ctenostome bryozoan which can be found on hydroid stems and other substrata.

DISTRIBUTION Records for this species are few, but specimens have been recorded on the whole coast of Norway. Further records include the Faeroe Islands and southern Greenland.

SIMILAR SPECIES *Goniodoris nodosa* (p. 52) is similar in shape and colour, but *L. danielsseni* is immediately recognisable by its unique jagged mantle edge.

KEY CHARACTERISTICS Mantle margin extended by spicule bundles to a serrated edge. Translucent white with yellow pigmented glandular structures in the post-branchial processes and the tips of the gill pinnae.

Adult, feeding on a bryozoan that is growing with small hydroids on the stems of the hydroid *Tubularia indivisa*, Gulen, Norway.

Studio shot of adult, Gulen, Norway.

Adult, with bryozoans on leg of sea spider, Gulen, Norway.

Okenia aspersa (Alder & Hancock, 1845)

DESCRIPTION The body of this nudibranch is translucent white in colour and is covered with yellow/orange, opaque white and brown speckling with a broad white stripe along the tail. There are 2 pairs of long, thin, anteriorly directed processes that precede the rhinophores. There are 5 pairs of processes arising from the mantle edge, becoming longer at the gill with the last 2 sharing a base. The long rhinophores are lamellate. *Okenia aspersa* may reach a length of 22 mm. The spawn consists of a short coil, like a spring, attached at one end to the substratum.

ECOLOGY This animal feeds on ascidians such as *Molgula* spp. and possibly also on other ascidians such as *Polycarpa* and *Ascidiella* species.

DISTRIBUTION Records for this species are few but specimens have been recorded all round Britain and Ireland, as far north as southern Norway and as far south as Arcachon on the Atlantic coast of France.

SIMILAR SPECIES *Okenia pulchella* (p. 62) is similar but has no bright yellow markings on the back and a different, more reticulated, appearance to the purple-brown pigment.

KEY CHARACTERISTICS Long processes arising from the mantle edge. Mottled brown and yellow pigment on body and processes.

Adult on silt covered bedrock, Rathlin Island, Northern Ireland.

Studio shot of adult, Tiree, west coast of Scotland.

Spawn coils on silty bedrock with the siphons of the ascidians *Polycarpa* sp. and *Molgula* sp. visible. Portrush, County Antrim, Ireland.

Okenia elegans (Leuckart, 1828)

DESCRIPTION The maximum recorded length of this attractive nudibranch is 80 mm. The body is white, suffused with pink in parts, varying to red in some individuals. Finger-like processes project from the head, the edges of the mantle and the middle of the dorsum. These processes are orange with yellow or white tips. There is a yellow band that runs around the edge of the foot. The lamellate rhinophores are rosy in colour with yellow tips. The spawn consists of an irregular and loosely coiled ribbon which varies in colour from pale pink to white.

ECOLOGY This nudibranch feeds on *Polycarpa* species ascidians. It is often found burrowed inside the test of the ascidian, with only its gills protruding.

DISTRIBUTION A scarce species in Britain and Ireland, *Okenia elegans* has been found at scattered localities from southwest England and Ireland to the west coast of Scotland.

SIMILAR SPECIES *Okenia leachii* (p. 60) is similar in size and shape, but has white coloration instead of yellow and red. Unlikely to be confused with other species.

KEY CHARACTERISTICS Long processes arising from the mantle edge and the midline of the back. White or red body with yellow-tipped processes.

Adult on gravel, Rathlin Island, Northern Ireland.

Studio shot of adult, Strangford Lough, Northern Ireland.

Adults and spawn, Sound of Jura, west coast of Scotland.

Okenia leachii

(Alder & Hancock, 1854)

DESCRIPTION *Okenia leachii* has a translucent body with a pinkish brown hue and long dorsal processes streaked with white pigment. The processes arise from the mantle rim and are in 3 rows down the back. The edge of the foot is also pigmented white, as are the rhinophore lamellae and the edges of the gills. Adults reach 40 mm in length. The spawn is a long sausage-shaped mass attached at one end by a filament.

ECOLOGY A rare species found on muddy sand seabeds usually in deep water, below 25 m. Probably feeds on burrowing sea squirts such as *Molgula occulta*.

DISTRIBUTION Originally described from four specimens, from Devon, Durham and the Hebrides; there are recent records from the Celtic Sea, and from the Shiant Isles and Skye on the west coast of Scotland. There are older records from the Shetlands, Connemara, and Norway.

SIMILAR SPECIES Living animals are easily distinguished from *Okenia elegans* (p. 58) by their colour; preserved animals can be distinguished by the 3 longitudinal rows of dorsal processes.

KEY CHARACTERISTICS Long processes arising from the mantle edge and in 3 rows on the back. Pigmented with white on the gills, edge of foot, and all processes.

Adult on shelly sand, Shiant Islands, west coast of Scotland.

Adult and spawn, Shiant Islands, west coast of Scotland.

Okenia elegans (p. 58) gills emerging from a sea squirt, Rathlin Island, Northern Ireland.

Okenia pulchella (Alder & Hancock, 1854)

DESCRIPTION The body of this nudibranch is translucent white in colour and is covered with cream and purple-brown speckling, with tiny spots of yellow. There are 2 pairs of long, thin, anteriorly directed processes that precede the rhinophores. Six finger-like processes arise from each side of the mantle edge. The long rhinophores are lamellate. *Okenia pulchella* may reach a length of 30 mm. The spawn consists of a long coil, like a spring, attached at one end to the substratum.

ECOLOGY This animal feeds on ascidians such as *Molgula occulta* or *Eugyra arenosa* buried below the surface of muddy sand, and the nudibranch may burrow completely inside the ascidian.

DISTRIBUTION Records for this species are few, but specimens have been collected recently in the Oban area of the west coast of Scotland, and there is a photographic record from the Mediterranean coast of France.

SIMILAR SPECIES *Okenia aspersa* (p. 56) is similar, but has small yellow patches on the back, sides and tail and opaque white pigment on the sides of the body and the middle of each gill.

KEY CHARACTERISTICS Long processes arising from the mantle edge. Mottled brown and cream pigment on body and processes.

Individual amongst sea squirts, Boddam Lighthouse, Peterhead, Scotland. (Chris Rickard)

Studio shot of adult, Luing, west coast of Scotland.

Spawn coils on muddy gravel, Luing, west coast of Scotland.

Trapania maculata

Haefelfinger, 1960

DESCRIPTION This animal may reach 17 mm in length. The body is white with characteristic yellow/orange patches. There is a curved, posteriorly directed, orange-tipped process at the base of each rhinophore and on either side of the branchial plume. The oral tentacles are long and streaked with orange pigment, and there is a pair of recurved propodial tentacles that are similarly pigmented. The lamellate rhinophores are yellow/orange in colour.

ECOLOGY All records of this species are from shallow water. *Trapania* species feed on kamptozoans (Entoprocta), which are tiny animals previously classified with the bryozoans, which live attached to the surface of sponges, bryozoans and hydroids.

DISTRIBUTION This is a rare southern species in Britain, recorded from the Lleyn peninsula in Wales and English Channel coasts. In Ireland it has been recorded from Connemara. Elsewhere it is known from the Brittany coast of France and the western Mediterranean.

SIMILAR SPECIES *Trapania tartanella* (p. 68) is similar but has no yellow or orange patches on the body. *Ancula cristata* (p. 48) is easily mistaken for this species, but has 2 processes directed forwards at the base of the rhinophores.

KEY CHARACTERISTICS The pattern of the yellow pigment on the body. Recurved yellow processes at the base of the rhinophores and alongside the gills.

Adult on tide-swept bedrock, Sark, Channel Islands.

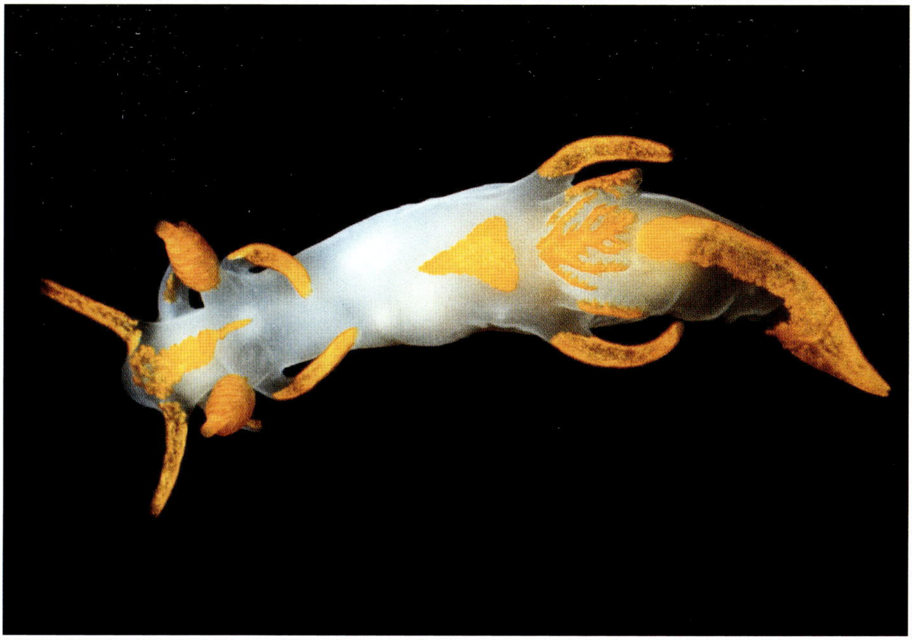

Studio shot of adult, Portland Bill, England.

Individual spawning, Mediterranean coast of Spain. (Enric Madrenas)

Trapania pallida

Kress, 1968

DESCRIPTION *Trapania pallida* is translucent white in colour with white patches on the rhinophores, processes, gills and tail. There are lateral processes directed posteriorly from the bases of the rhinophores and another pair alongside the gills, similar to *Trapania maculata*; however in *T. pallida* they are shorter. The maximum recorded length for this species is 15 mm.

ECOLOGY The prey species of *T. pallida* appears to be a kamptozoan, possibly a species of *Loxocalyx*. It is usually found amongst bryozoans, hydroids and sponges on rocky sublittoral cliffs and outcrops, in depths of 10–20 metres.

DISTRIBUTION Records of this scarce species are from the west coast of Ireland, Loch Sunart in western Scotland, the Isle of Man, southwest England, and from the Atlantic coasts of France and Spain. The suggested conspecificity with *Trapania lineata* on the basis of similar COI sequences is dismissed here because of differences in distribution and morphology of these species and 2% difference in the COI barcode.

SIMILAR SPECIES This is the only *Trapania* species in the northeast Atlantic with white, rather than yellow or orange, pigment.

KEY CHARACTERISTICS The pattern of the white pigment on the body. Recurved processes at the base of the rhinophores and alongside the gills.

Adult on silty bedrock, Sark, Channel Islands.

Studio shot of adult, Connemara, Ireland.

On coralline encrusted bedrock, Connemara, Ireland.

Trapania tartanella (Ihering, 1886)

DESCRIPTION The body is translucent white with no markings apart from a yellow patch at the tail. The white viscera are clearly visible. There is a curved, posteriorly directed process at the base of each rhinophore and on either side of the branchial plume. The oral tentacles are long and there is a pair of recurved propodial tentacles. All these processes and the tips of the gills are coloured with yellow surface pigment which becomes orange at the tips. The lamellate rhinophores are yellow/orange in colour. This animal may reach 20 mm in length.

ECOLOGY *Trapania* species feed on kamptozoans, which are tiny animals previously classified with the bryozoans, which live attached to the surface of sponges, bryozoans and hydroids.

DISTRIBUTION This species has only recently been discovered in Britain, in Cornwall and at Skomer Island in Wales. Elsewhere it is known from the Atlantic coasts of Spain and Portugal.

SIMILAR SPECIES *Trapania maculata* (p. 64) is similar but has orange patches on the body. In southern Spain *Trapania hispalensis* (not included here) is almost identical but has no gradation of colour in the yellow processes. *Ancula cristata* (p. 48) is similar in colour, but has 2 processes extending forward from the base of the rhinophore instead of the single curved process behind the rhinophores.

KEY CHARACTERISTICS Yellow pigment grading to orange on the tips of all the extremities. Recurved yellow processes at the base of the rhinophores and alongside the gills.

Two adults on the sponge *Haliclona* sp., Sesimbra, Portugal.

Studio shot of adult, Plymouth, England.

Individual spawning, Torbay, England. (Terry Griffiths)

Aegires punctilucens (Orbigny, 1837)

DESCRIPTION This animal is usually 10–20 mm in length. It is very inconspicuous, brown (rarely white) in colour, but can be easily identified by the many knob-shaped tubercles and the tiny iridescent blue spots scattered over the back of the animal. The oral tentacles are short and rounded and the rhinophores are smooth. The rhinophores emerge from sheaths with large papillae at their edges.

ECOLOGY *Aegires punctilucens* is well camouflaged amongst its food, the calcareous sponge *Leucosolenia botryoides*, and may be hidden inside a clump of the sponge.

DISTRIBUTION Occurs around the coasts of Britain, Ireland, and Norway and south to the Mediterranean.

SIMILAR SPECIES This nudibranch is unlike any others in the northeast Atlantic, but there are similar species in the Pacific Ocean.

KEY CHARACTERISTICS Iridescent blue spots on the mantle. Knob-shaped mantle tubercles. Smooth rhinophores, unusual for a dorid.

Adult on silty *Modiolus modiolus* shell, Strangford Lough, Northern Ireland.

Studio shot of adult, Strangford Lough, Northern Ireland.

Two individuals camouflaged on the sponge *Leucosolenia botryoides*, Skomer, Wales.

Colga villosa (Odhner, 1907)

DESCRIPTION The body is translucent white and may reach a length of up to 65 mm. The mantle is covered with elongate pointed processes which are scattered over the back and in lines at the edge of the mantle rim. These processes are more closely packed across the front of the head. The oral tentacles are broad, and there are 7 tripinnate gills. The rhinophores have about 20 lamellae and are milky white.

ECOLOGY Found on mixed bottoms of rock, stones and shells amongst hydroids, bryozoans, and ascidians from shallow water to 300 m depth. The food is unknown, but probably a bryozoan, possibly *Dendrobeania murrayana*.

DISTRIBUTION *Colga villosa* is only found in Arctic waters in northern Norway. Further distribution includes Svalbard and Greenland.

SIMILAR SPECIES No other species in the region has a mantle with multiple, white-tipped processes at the edge.

KEY CHARACTERISTICS White, pointed, unbranched processes all over mantle surface. Oral veil with many pointed processes.

Adult feeding on the bryozoan *Dendrobeania murrayana*, northern Norway. (Erling Svensen)

Northern Norway. (Erling Svensen)

Northern Norway. (Erling Svensen)

Crimora papillata

Alder & Hancock, 1862

DESCRIPTION The body is translucent white and may reach a length of up to 35 mm. Small, forked, bristly processes, scattered all over the body, make it easy to identify. These bristles are yellow/orange in colour. The oral tentacles are short and similarly pigmented. The rhinophores are lamellate and their tips are covered with yellow pigment.

ECOLOGY Usually closely associated with the bryozoan species *Chartella papyracea* but also found on *Flustra foliacea* or *Securiflustra securifrons*.

DISTRIBUTION *Crimora papillata* is only found sublittorally, to the south and west of Britain, but extends up the Irish west coast as far as Rathlin Island and also to St. Kilda, off the west coast of Scotland. It is now well established in southern Norway. Further distribution includes the Mediterranean.

SIMILAR SPECIES The branched orange or yellow processes are unique to this species.

KEY CHARACTERISTICS Branched yellow processes all over mantle surface.

Two adults feeding on the bryozoan *Flustra foliacea*, Calf of Man, Isle of Man.

Studio shot, Skomer, Wales.

Two adults and two spawn coils on the bryozoan *Securiflustra securifrons*, Rathlin Island, Northern Ireland.

Kaloplocamus cf. *ramosus* (Cantraine, 1835)

DESCRIPTION The body is translucent white and may reach a length of up to 45 mm. The mantle is slightly tuberculate and has a series of small orange spots along each side. The mantle rim bears 5 processes with branched tips. One process is next to the rhinophores, 3 along the side of the body, a fourth alongside the gills and the fifth behind the gills. There is an orange glandular structure at the base of the branched part of the process. The oral veil bears numerous branched processes across the front of the head. There are 7 tripinnate gills. The rhinophores have many lamellae and are greenish white.

ECOLOGY Found in trawl samples in the English Channel and Bay of Biscay at 110 m depth. Likely to be associated with a bryozoan but the diet is not known.

DISTRIBUTION DNA evidence indicates that *Kaloplocamus ramosus* is a species complex, reported from the Mediterranean Sea, the Azores and Australia to Hong Kong. Mediterranean specimens are translucent orange in colour.

SIMILAR SPECIES This species bears a superficial resemblance to a *Dendronotus* species (pp. 160–168) because of its branched processes, but has a dorsal ring of gills like all dorids.

KEY CHARACTERISTICS Branched processes arise from the mantle margin. Oral veil with many branched processes.

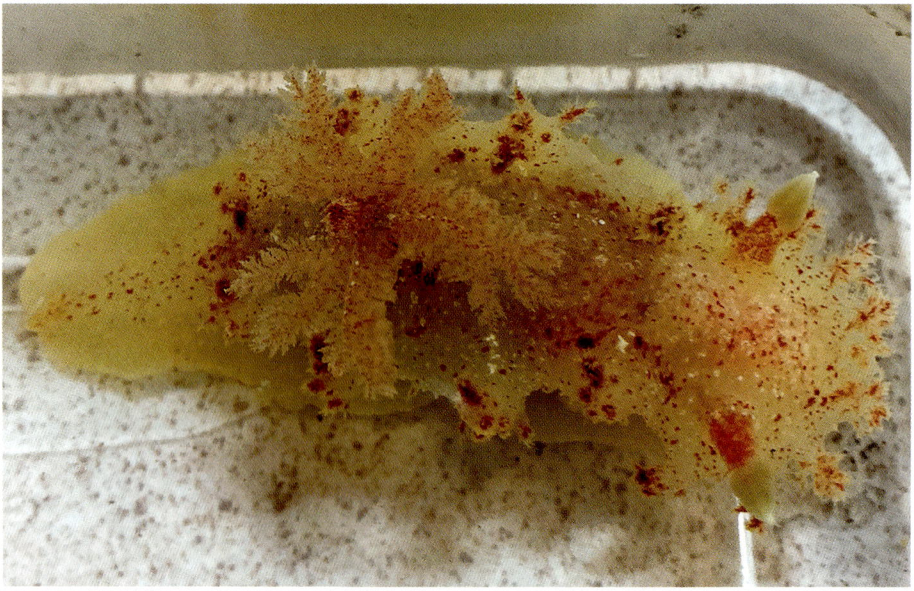

Approximately 100 km south of Cork, Ireland (80 m depth). (Hayden Close/CEFAS)

Greilada elegans Bergh, 1894

DESCRIPTION This distinctive species is orange in colour with brilliant blue iridescent spots. The gills are robust with iridescent blue-green lines along their ribs. The head may bear up to 22 finger-like processes. The maximum recorded length for this species is 48 mm.

ECOLOGY *Greilada elegans* feeds preferentially on the bryozoan species *Bugula turbinata* but has also been reported to feed on other species of *Bugula*.

DISTRIBUTION Records of this species are from Kilkieran Bay, County Galway; Sheep Haven, County Donegal; Skomer Island, Pembrokeshire; Lundy, South Cornwall; Azores and the Mediterranean. Appears to be very sporadic, disappearing from areas where it was common for several years and not seen in Britain or Ireland for 30 years.

SIMILAR SPECIES The spectacular colour of this nudibranch readily distinguishes it from any other in Britain and Ireland.

KEY CHARACTERISTICS Orange coloration with large iridescent blue spots. Rhinophores and gills without sheaths or accessory processes.

Adults on the bryozoan *Crisularia plumosa*, Milford Haven, Wales.

Limacia clavigera (O F Müller, 1776)

DESCRIPTION *Limacia clavigera* may grow to 20 mm in length. It is white with yellow-orange tipped processes around its body. The processes at the front have rough surfaces and are held horizontally. Those at the sides of the body are smooth and are normally curved upwards over the dorsum. There are slightly raised orange spots on the animal's back. The rhinophores are lamellate and they are also tipped with yellow pigment.

ECOLOGY A common species which feeds preferentially on the bryozoan *Electra pilosa* usually on red algae in the shallow sublittoral. Individuals may also be found feeding on other bryozoans beneath rocks in the intertidal and on bryozoan encrusted stones in tide races.

DISTRIBUTION This species is distributed around Britain and Ireland and from Norway to Portugal. Mediterranean specimens are now known to be *Limacia inesae* (not included here), and this species seems to overlap with *L. clavigera* on the Portuguese coast. *L. inesae* has a single row of orange tubercles down the midline of the back.

SIMILAR SPECIES *L. clavigera* can be distinguished from the many other white and orange or yellow species by the presence of processes all along the edge of the mantle.

KEY CHARACTERISTICS Long, orange-tipped processes around the edge of the mantle. Three small gills and orange tubercles on the back.

Adult feeding on the bryozoan *Electra pilosa* growing on the red seaweed *Delesseria sanguinea*, Skomer, Wales.

Studio shot of adult, Gulen, Norway.

Spiral of spawn on kelp blade, Gulen, Norway.

Palio dubia

(M Sars, 1829)

DESCRIPTION The body of *Palio dubia* is brownish green with numerous rounded white or yellow tubercles. There are short white papillae on either side of the gills. This animal may grow to a length of 29 mm.

ECOLOGY *P. dubia* is only found sublittorally from depths of 10 to 100 m. It feeds on the bryozoan species *Eucratea loricata*.

DISTRIBUTION A northern species in Britain and Ireland, but records have in the past been mixed with *Palio nothus* which has a wider distribution. Reliable records are from Belfast Lough, Loch Etive and the Oban area, and off Northumberland. Further distribution includes Norway as far north as the Lofoten Islands and the New England coast of America.

SIMILAR SPECIES *P. dubia* has been frequently confused with *P. nothus* (p. 82) but differs in having rounded rather than pointed tubercles on the body, and even rather than blotchy, green coloration.

KEY CHARACTERISTICS Yellow, rounded tubercles on the yellow-green body. The rhinophores of *P. dubia* are shorter and bear more lamellae than those of *P. nothus*.

Adult on the bryozoan *Eucratea loricata*, southern Denmark.

Adult on red seaweed, Bodø, Norway.

Spawn coil, Belfast Lough, Northern Ireland.

Palio nothus

(Johnston, 1838)

DESCRIPTION The body is blackish green with pale patches. The mantle tubercles are conical in shape. There are short club-shaped papillae on either side of the gills. The largest recorded specimen was 20 mm in length. The spawn is white or pale pink in colour and forms a coiled ribbon.

ECOLOGY This species occurs under rocks on the low shore and in the shallow subtidal. It preys upon the finely branching ctenostome bryozoans *Amathia* species.

DISTRIBUTION *Palio nothus* can be found around Britain and Ireland and north to Trondheim Fjord in Norway. On the French Atlantic coast this species is scarce, but it has been recorded as far south as Mediterranean coast of Spain where it is more often seen at night, in shallow water.

SIMILAR SPECIES *Palio dubia* (p. 80) has been confused with this species in the past.

KEY CHARACTERISTICS Transparent, conulose tubercles on the body. Rhinophores with long shafts and few lamellae.

Two adults on silt-covered bryozoans, Strangford Lough, Northern Ireland.

Studio shot of adult, Strangford Lough, Northern Ireland.

Studio shot of adult and spawn, Portrush, Northern Ireland.

Polycera capitata (Alder & Hancock, 1854)

Synonym *Polycera norvegica* (Sørensen *et al.*, 2020)

DESCRIPTION The body of this nudibranch is translucent white with patches of yellow pigment forming longitudinal lines. Some individuals have fine black spots over the body. There are usually 4 or 6 oral veil processes. At either side of the branchial plume there is a single orange-tipped process. The tips of the rhinophores, propodial tentacles, oral lobes and gills are pigmented yellow. The rhinophores have 8–11 lamellae. The maximum recorded length for this species is 15 mm. The spawn is a short, white, curved ribbon.

ECOLOGY Feeds on *Membranipora membranacea*, a bryozoan species that grows on kelp, and also on other bryozoans such as *Electra pilosa* on red algae. It is often found in large numbers.

DISTRIBUTION Appears to be a warmer water species than *Polycera quadrilineata*. Common on western coasts of Britain and Ireland and from southern Norway to the Mediterranean.

SIMILAR SPECIES Previously synonymised with *P. quadrilineata* (p. 90) and not all individuals are distinguishable from that species. Populations of *Polycera capitata* usually contain colour morphs which include black-speckled individuals and others with pale primrose yellow pigment and brown patches. The best distinguishing feature is the rhinophore shape and number of lamellae.

KEY CHARACTERISTICS Four processes on the oral veil, 2 rhinophores without basal processes. White with yellow processes and body has short yellow spots. Post-branchial appendages cylindrical with orange tips.

Adult feeding on the bryozoan *Electra pilosa* growing on the red seaweed *Calliblepharis ciliata*, Skomer, Wales.

Studio shot of adult, Mullaghmore, County Sligo, Ireland.

Spawn on red seaweed with the bryozoan *Electra pilosa*, Mullaghmore, County Sligo, Ireland.

Polycera faeroensis

Lemche, 1929

DESCRIPTION This nudibranch may grow to a length of 45 mm; the ground colour is translucent white. Eight or more yellow-tipped oral veil processes are present. There is a yellow tipped process at either side of the gills, which is usually flattened with several points. The tips of the rhinophores, propodial tentacles, oral lobes and gills are also pigmented with yellow. There is usually some yellow pigment on the vestigial mantle edge between the oral processes and the post-branchial processes, and this can be a continuous line in heavily pigmented specimens. Some individuals have extensive large yellow spots along the midline of the body between the rhinophores and gill cluster and on the sides of the body. The spawn is a white coiled ribbon.

ECOLOGY It appears that *Polycera faeroensis* feeds on erect bryozoans such as *Caberea ellisii, Scrupocellaria scruposa, Bugula purpurotincta* and other *Bugula* species.

DISTRIBUTION A common species in the circalittoral and on steep rock faces on the northern and western coasts of Britain and Ireland. Originally described from the Faeroes, this is predominantly a cold-water species, being found in open coast sites as far south as Portugal.

SIMILAR SPECIES *Polycera kernowensis* (p. 88) is very similar but has only one point on the post-branchial processes and never has yellow pigment on the body apart from a stripe on the tail.

KEY CHARACTERISTICS Eight or more processes on the oral veil, rhinophores without basal processes. Mantle edge developed into a flap with multiple points alongside the gill cluster. White with yellow processes and often with yellow spots on the body.

Adult on bedrock with bryozoans, Rathlin Island, Northern Ireland.

Studio shot of adult, Skomer, Wales.

Spawn on the red seaweed *Heterosiphonia plumosa*, Copelands, Northern Ireland.

Polycera kernowensis Korshunova, Driessen, Picton & Martynov, 2021

DESCRIPTION This nudibranch may grow to a length of 30 mm, the ground colour is translucent white. Eight or more yellow tipped oral veil processes are present. There is a yellow-tipped process at either side of the gills. The tips of the rhinophores, propodial tentacles, oral lobes and gills are also pigmented with yellow. The spawn is a white coiled ribbon.

ECOLOGY It appears that *Polycera kernowensis* feeds on erect bryozoans such as *Bicellariella ciliata, Bugula turbinata* and perhaps other *Bugula* and *Crisia* species.

DISTRIBUTION A common species in the circalittoral and on steep rock faces on the western and southern coasts of Britain and Ireland. Rare in southern Norway but more common in western Ireland, southwest England, and northern France.

SIMILAR SPECIES Only separated from *Polycera faeroensis* (p. 86) in 2021 after DNA analysis (Korshunova *et al.*, 2021). It differs from *P. faeroensis* in having only a single point to the processes alongside the gills and no yellow pigment on the mantle. There are several other species in the family Goniodorididae, as well as *Polycera,* which have similar colouring, such as *Ancula cristata* (p. 48).

KEY CHARACTERISTICS Eight or more processes on the oral veil, rhinophores without basal processes. Mantle edge developed into a single process alongside the gill cluster. White with yellow processes and without yellow spots on the body.

Amongst jewel anemones *Corynactis viridis* and bryozoans, Connemara, Ireland.

Studio shot of adult, Skomer, Wales.

Two adults and spawn on the bryozoan *Crisularia plumosa*, Portrush, Northern Ireland.

Polycera quadrilineata (O F Müller, 1776)

DESCRIPTION The body of this nudibranch is usually translucent white with patches of yellow pigment forming a mid-dorsal row of spots, broken lines along the vestigial mantle margin and lines of spots on the sides of the body. A number of colour morphs exist which include grey or black longitudinal broken lines between the yellow markings and individuals with scattered large orange spots. There are usually 4 or 6 oral veil processes. At either side of the branchial plume there is a single yellow-tipped process. The tips of the rhinophores, propodial tentacles, oral lobes and gills are pigmented yellow and there is often black pigment on the rhinophore clavus (stem). The rhinophores have 11–17 lamellae. The maximum recorded length for this species is 45 mm. The spawn is a narrow ribbon of one overlapping turn.

ECOLOGY Feeds on encrusting and erect bryozoans including *Cradoscrupocellaria reptans*, *Membranipora membranacea*, *Electra pilosa*. It is often found in large numbers.

DISTRIBUTION Common around Britain and Ireland, and from Norway to the Mediterranean.

SIMILAR SPECIES Sometimes *Polycera quadrilineata* is confused with *Polycera faeroensis* (p. 86); however, in the latter there are 8 or more oral veil processes. The distinct species status of *Polycera capitata* (p. 84) has only recently been recognised. Some colour morphs are indistinguishable, but populations of *P. capitata* include individuals with black speckles, and this species has more rounded rhinophore bulbs with only 8–11 lamellae.

KEY CHARACTERISTICS Four processes on the oral veil, 2 rhinophores without basal processes. White with yellow processes and body has elongate yellow spots. Post-branchial appendages with yellow tips, bases often flattened with many white glands.

Adult on the red seaweed *Delesseria sanguinea*, Isle of Man.

Studio shot of the adult, Isle of Man.

Spawn coil on red algae, Skomer, Wales.

Thecacera pennigera (Montagu, 1813)

DESCRIPTION *Thecacera pennigera* may grow to a length of 30 mm. The body is translucent white in colour with tiny orange, yellow and black spots (the orange spots are usually larger than the black ones). The flared rhinophore sheaths are unusual in that they do not completely encircle the rhinophores but rather they envelop them. The branchial plume is arranged in the shape of a horseshoe. Alongside the gills there is a pair of glandular processes that are defensive in function.

ECOLOGY This animal feeds on the bryozoan *Bugula plumosa*; often it is inconspicuous in its natural habitat due to the disruptive camouflage of the orange and black spots. The untidy, narrow, white ribbons of spawn are often the best clue to its presence.

DISTRIBUTION Occurs in the south and west of Britain and Ireland, extending along the English Channel to the Isle of Wight and up the west coast of Ireland as far as Portrush, County Antrim. Also recorded on Atlantic coasts of France, Spain and Portugal to the Mediterranean.

SIMILAR SPECIES The black-spotted form of *Polycera capitata* (p. 84) has been mistaken for *T. pennigera* but the lack of rhinophore sheaths in *P. capitata* should rule out this error.

KEY CHARACTERISTICS Rhinophores with incomplete sheaths. White with orange and black spots.

Adult feeding on the bryozoan *Crisularia plumosa*, Sark, Channel Islands.

Studio shot, Skomer, Wales.

Spawn ribbon on the bryozoan *Crisularia plumosa*, Skomer, Wales.

Cadlina laevis

(Linnaeus, 1767)

DESCRIPTION This species is white or translucent white in colour; occasionally there is a yellow border around the edge of the mantle. The mantle tubercles are very short. One of the most characteristic features are the white or lemon-yellow glands situated towards the mantle margin. Mature specimens may reach 32 mm in length.

ECOLOGY Feeds on sponges such as *Halisarca dujardini* and *Dysidea fragilis. Cadlina laevis* is one of the few British nudibranchs which have direct development, with tiny juvenile slugs hatching from the eggs rather than veliger larvae.

DISTRIBUTION *C. laevis* has a wide-ranging distribution; it is known from eastern America, Greenland, Iceland and from Norway to Spain.

SIMILAR SPECIES *Cadlina pellucida* (p. 96) is similar but with brown rhinophores and gills. *Aldisa zetlandica* (p. 98) is another white dorid, but it has a much thicker body and larger tubercles.

KEY CHARACTERISTICS Flat oval body with small gills which retract into a pocket. Defensive white or lemon-yellow glands around the edge of the mantle.

Adult on coralline encrusted bedrock, Mayo, Ireland.

Studio shot of adult, Connemara, Ireland.

Two adults with spawn coil, Horten, Oslo Fjord, Norway. (Roy Dahl)

Cadlina pellucida (Risso, 1826)

DESCRIPTION This species is white or translucent white in colour with mantle tubercles which are very short. The gills and rhinophores are dark brown. As with other *Cadlina* species there are white glands beneath the skin near the mantle margin. Mature specimens may reach 20 mm in length.

ECOLOGY Reported to feed on the sponges *Spongia lamella* and *Dysidea* species.

DISTRIBUTION *Cadlina pellucida* was first seen on the British coast in 2012, with a few records since, all on the southwest coast of England. It occurs on Atlantic coasts of France, Spain, Portugal and in the Mediterranean Sea.

SIMILAR SPECIES *Cadlina laevis* (p. 94) is similar but with white rhinophores and gills.

KEY CHARACTERISTICS Flat oval body with small gills which retract into a pocket. Defensive white glands under the skin near the edge of the mantle.

Lateral view of *Cadlina pellucida*, Ushant, Brittany, France. (François Roche)

Close-up photograph of an individual, beneath a rock, Costa Brava, Spain. (Enric Madrenas)

Two individuals with a spawn coil on the sponge *Spongia lamella*, Setubal, Portugal. (J.P. Silva)

Aldisa zetlandica

(Alder & Hancock, 1854)

DESCRIPTION The mantle of *Aldisa zetlandica* is usually white (has been reported as greenish grey) in colour and bears rounded tubercles. The gills and rhinophores are white in colour. The sides of the foot are tall and the gut may show through the foot as a purple mass. The gills are bushy and fully retractile into a pocket. Individuals may reach a length of up to 35 mm.

ECOLOGY A sublittoral species known originally from dredging in deep water in Shetland. Recent finds have been in sponge rich areas amongst a variety of axinellid sponges, usually below 25 m depth. It feeds on red and blue species of *Hymedesmia*.

DISTRIBUTION A rare species reported from Shetland to the Azores. Recent finds in Britain and Ireland have been from Achill Island and Skird Rocks in Galway, where it has been collected on several occasions. It is frequent in some locations in southern Norway.

SIMILAR SPECIES The only other white dorid likely to be confused with this species is *Cadlina laevis* (p. 94) which is much flatter in profile. Small individuals could be confused with *Adalaria* species (pp. 22–24) or *Onchidoris muricata* (p. 40), but these species have separately contractile gills and no true gill pocket.

KEY CHARACTERISTICS White body with rounded profile. Five bushy gills.

Adult on bedrock with the blue sponge *Hymedesmia paupertas*, Gulen, Norway.

Adult on bedrock with coralline algae, Egersund, Norway. (Erling Svensen)

Spawn coil on bedrock with coralline algae, Egersund, Norway. (Erling Svensen)

Felimida krohnii (Vérany, 1846)

DESCRIPTION This chromodorid can reach a length of 45 mm, but most are up to 30 mm. The body and foot are pink to purple and translucent with 3 longitudinal lines which may be white or yellow. The yellow may be edged with white and the lines may be broken. One line runs from in front of the rhinophores to the gill pocket while the others run along the sides of the mantle starting a small distance behind the rhinophores and joining behind the gill pocket. Larger individuals develop spots in the space between these lines. A yellow band runs along the edge of the mantle with a diffuse blue band inside this. The rhinophores are dark purple with up to 20 lamellae. There are 5–9 unipinnate gill leaflets.

ECOLOGY Observed feeding on both pink and yellow species of the keratose sponge *Aplysilla*. Found under rocks and in dark places on rocky substrata.

DISTRIBUTION Recently found on the southwest coast of England and distributed on the Atlantic coasts of France, Spain and Portugal. Frequent in the Mediterranean Sea where it is common in the western basin and present but rare as far east as Crete.

SIMILAR SPECIES There are several other *Felimida* species in northern Spain and further south (not included here), but none have the 3 longitudinal lines of *Felimida krohnii*.

KEY CHARACTERISTICS Pale pink-purple body with 3 yellow or white longitudinal lines.

Mating pair of animals, Hand Deeps, Plymouth, England. (Tamsyn Mann)

Large individual with well-developed colouring between the dorsal lines of pigment, Mediterranean Coast of Spain. (Enric Madrenas)

Mature individual in the process of laying a spawn coil, Mediterranean Coast of Spain. (Enric Madrenas)

Atagema gibba

Pruvot-Fol, 1951

DESCRIPTION The body is chocolate brown in colour. The mantle bears numerous small white tubercles that form a reticulate pattern of ridges. The rhinophores have distinctive trumpet shaped sheaths. Grows to at least 68 mm in length. The spawn consists of a ruffled yellow ribbon of eggs deposited in a spiral of one and a half turns.

ECOLOGY A sponge-eating dorid which has been found on steep rockfaces in about 8–15 metres depth. Thought to feed on the sponge *Haliclona fibulata*.

DISTRIBUTION This species is rare and the only British records are from The Lizard peninsula in Cornwall and the east coast of St. Mary's in the Isles of Scilly. There are also records from the Channel coast of France and Banyuls-sur-Mer on the Mediterranean coast.

SIMILAR SPECIES Easily distinguished from other large sponge-eating dorids by the sheaths around the rhinophores and the ridge along the back.

KEY CHARACTERISTICS Brown dorid with ridge along centre of back. Sheaths around the rhinophores. Distinctive reticulate pattern of tubercles.

Adult feeding on the sponge *Haliclona fibulata*, Isles of Scilly, England.

Adult on bedrock with jewel anemones, Isles of Scilly, England.

Yellow ribbon of spawn, Isles of Scilly, England.

Aporodoris millegrana (Alder & Hancock, 1854)

DESCRIPTION This dorid nudibranch is very flattened and a dark purple-brown in colour. The mantle is densely covered with small, rounded, spiculose tubercles. The rhinophores have low sheaths surrounding their bases and a ring of small tubercles at the edge of these sheaths. Adults reach 30 mm in length.

ECOLOGY Found beneath rocks in the shallow sublittoral. The food, presumably a sponge, has not been determined.

DISTRIBUTION This species was described from two specimens collected near Torbay but has not subsequently been reported from the British Isles. It occurs on the French Atlantic coast, Portugal and the coasts of Spain and France in the Mediterranean Sea.

SIMILAR SPECIES The flat body shape, small uniform-sized tubercles and purple-brown colour are distinctive.

KEY CHARACTERISTICS Flattened purple-brown dorid nudibranch. Many small tubercles cover the mantle.

Resting animal on rock with calcareous algae, Mediterranean coast of Spain. (Enric Madrenas)

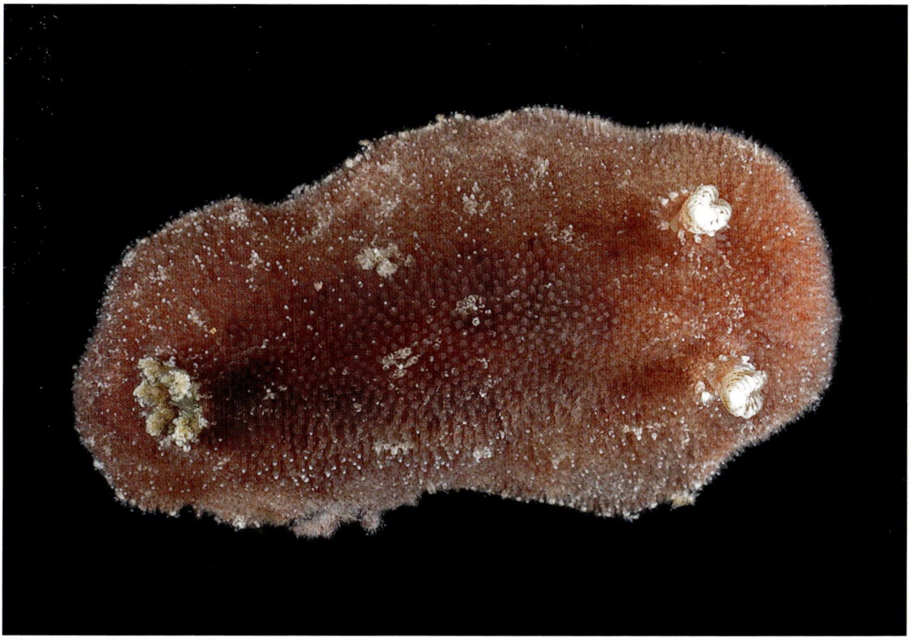

Typical coloration of an adult, Mediterranean coast of Spain. (Enric Madrenas)

Animal on bryozoans, Mediterranean coast of Spain. (Enric Madrenas)

Discodoris rosi

Ortea, 1979

DESCRIPTION A somewhat flattened dorid which ranges in colour from yellow to orange-red and has white rings on the surface. The mantle is rough and densely covered with small even-sized tubercles. When extended the gills form a neat, globular cluster. Adults reach 30 mm in length.

HABITAT Rocky reefs in the sublittoral. Feeds on orange or red microcionid sponges including *Microciona strepsitoxa*.

DISTRIBUTION In Britain this species was first found in 2002 at Penzance in Cornwall, with more records from the Scilly Isles in 2008. It occurs on the French Atlantic coast and the coasts of Spain and France in the Mediterranean and as far east as Slovenia.

SIMILAR SPECIES Could be confused with *Rostanga rubra* (p. 114) but has a broader body shape and different markings.

KEY CHARACTERISTICS Flattened orange or yellow dorid nudibranch. White rings form a pattern on the back.

Adult on shelly gravel, Sesimbra, Portugal.

Studio shot of adult, Vigo, Spain.

Adult and two orange ribbons of spawn, Porthkerris, Cornwall, England. (Hazel Selley)

Geitodoris planata (Alder & Hancock, 1846)

DESCRIPTION Adults may reach a length of up to 65 mm. The body of this nudibranch is mottled with brown, orange or purple. There may be up to 12 stellate patches on the mantle that radiate from a central papilla; these patches are paler in colour than the rest of the dorsum and correspond to acid glands. The back of this animal is covered with numerous small tubercles. The spawn is a broad ribbon laid in a spiral with the upper edge neatly rippled or convoluted.

ECOLOGY Usually found in the shallow subtidal, it feeds on mycalid sponges such as *Mycale rotalis, M. contarenii* and *M. similaris.*

DISTRIBUTION Locally common on the south and west coasts of Britain and Ireland including the Western Isles of Scotland and the Isle of Man; and from Norway to the Mediterranean. It suddenly appeared in the Netherlands in 1999 and underwent a population explosion there in 2001.

SIMILAR SPECIES In the past this species has been confused with *Archidoris pseudoargus* (p. 118); however, it can be readily distinguished by the presence of brown spots on the underside of the mantle. A very similar species, *Discodoris stellifera*, is present in Portugal and the Mediterranean (not included here).

KEY CHARACTERISTICS Long finger-like oral tentacles, not present in *A. pseudoargus.* Stellate shaped patches surrounding large tubercles on the mantle.

Two adults mating, Kilkieran Bay, County Galway, Ireland.

Adult amongst shell and stones, Skomer Island, Wales.

Large ribbon of spawn amongst bryozoans, Skomer Island, Wales.

Jorunna artsdatabankia

Neuhaus, Rauch, Bakken, Picton, Pola & Malaquias, 2021

DESCRIPTION This species of *Jorunna* is recently described (Neuhaus *et al.*, 2021) and is subtly different in coloration from other *Jorunna* species in the area. The mantle is velvety in appearance and plain pale yellow to beige in colour with a small number of contrasting dark brown markings. Individuals may reach a length of up to 55 mm. The spawn is a broad ribbon with a fluted edge laid in a neat, tight coil.

ECOLOGY This species has only been found in the circalittoral zone in sponge rich habitats. It feeds on the sponge *Haliclona urceolus*.

DISTRIBUTION Currently thought to be a northern species with records from Northern Ireland, western Scotland, and southern Norway.

SIMILAR SPECIES Other species of *Jorunna* in the area have mottled coloration.

KEY CHARACTERISTICS Mantle covered with even spiculose velvety tubercles. Plain beige in colour with a few dark spots.

Adult on silty bedrock, Loch Crinan, west coast of Scotland.

Adult on silty bedrock with a chewed sponge *Haliclona urceolus*, Loch Caolisport, Scotland.

Spawn coil on red algae, Rathlin Island, Northern Ireland.

Jorunna tomentosa

(Cuvier, 1804)

DESCRIPTION *Jorunna tomentosa* is grey, beige, or sandy brown in colour. The mantle is velvety in appearance and to the touch with a mottled, sponge-like appearance. This effect is created by the presence of numerous, small, uniform tubercles. Often there are several pairs of dark brown spots on the sides of the mantle. Individuals may reach a length of up to 55 mm. DNA evidence shows that this is an unresolved species complex, but no external characters are known to identify the component species. The spawn is a broad ribbon laid in a neat, tight coil.

ECOLOGY This animal may be found on the shore and in the shallow subtidal. It feeds on a variety of sponges, but especially on species of *Haliclona* including *Haliclona oculata* and *Haliclona cinerea*.

DISTRIBUTION Found around Britain and Ireland and from the Faeroes to the Mediterranean.

SIMILAR SPECIES This name is currently in use for a species complex.

KEY CHARACTERISTICS Mantle covered with even spiculose velvety tubercles. Plain beige or grey in colour with a few dark spots.

Adult feeding on *Haliclona cinerea*, Moray, Scotland.

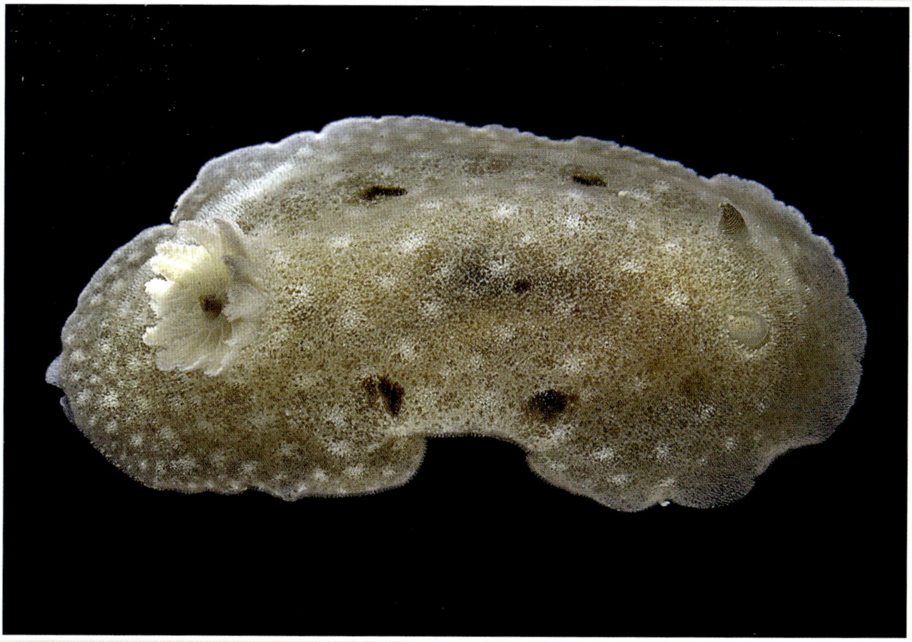

Studio shot of adult, Connemara, Ireland.

Ribbon of spawn on silty bedrock, Connemara, Ireland.

Rostanga rubra (Risso, 1818)

DESCRIPTION The colour of this nudibranch varies from bright red to pale orange-yellow with tiny black spots scattered on its dorsum. The mantle bears many minute tubercles and defensive spicules. There is a characteristic pale patch between the rhinophores. Adults may attain a body length of up to 15 mm.

ECOLOGY Most often found on the low shore or in the shallow subtidal. On shore it normally feeds upon the red sponge *Ophlitaspongia papilla*. In the sublittoral it has normally been found eating *Microciona atrasanguinea*. At St. Kilda it was found feeding on *Ophlitaspongia kildensis* in the sublittoral.

DISTRIBUTION *Rostanga rubra* has been found around the Orkneys and at St. Abbs Head on the North Sea coast as well as on the south and west coasts of Britain and Ireland. Further distribution from Norway south to the Mediterranean. Possibly a species complex.

SIMILAR SPECIES Unlikely to be confused with other British dorids except perhaps with the red variety of *Archidoris pseudoargus* (p. 118). *Discodoris rosi* (p. 106) is another red dorid; it grows to a much larger size than *Rostanga rubra* and has rings of white pigment on the back.

KEY CHARACTERISTICS Red dorid with paler patch between rhinophores. Gills small, held in a neat vertical cup.

Two adults on the sponge *Microciona atrasanguinea*, Strangford Lough, Northern Ireland.

Studio shot of adult, Strangford Lough, Northern Ireland.

Adult and spawn on *Microciona atrasanguinea*, Strangford Lough, Northern Ireland.

Thordisa azmanii

Cervera & García-Gómez, 1989

DESCRIPTION This nudibranch is brown to orange in colour with a paler mantle margin. The mantle is evenly covered with tubercles which are mostly rounded but include taller, more angular tubercles which may coalesce into a ridge in the middle of the back. The rhinophores are lamellate, with 10–12 lamellae and are brown with light brown tips. There are 7 bipinnate gills which are fully retractile and similar in colour to the rhinophores. Adults may attain a body length of up to 15 mm.

ECOLOGY Feeds on the sponges *Raspailia hispida* and *Raspailia ramosa*.

DISTRIBUTION Very rare in southern England where it has only been seen once, at the Isles of Scilly. This species was described from the intertidal region in the Strait of Gibraltar and has been seen at sites on the Spanish Atlantic coast.

SIMILAR SPECIES The dorsal papillae of this species are distinctively different from any other species known from the area.

KEY CHARACTERISTICS Orange-brown dorid with paler tips to larger tubercles, rhinophores and gill leaflets. Gills well-spaced out when expanded, not forming a cup.

One adult on silty rock next to the sponge *Raspailia ramosa*, Isles of Scilly, England.

Studio shot of adult, Isles of Scilly, England.

Two spawn coils on the sponge *Raspailia ramosa*, Isles of Scilly, England.

Archidoris pseudoargus (Rapp, 1827)

DESCRIPTION This is one of the most common nudibranchs found on British shores and in many places, it is known as the 'sea lemon'. The mantle bears many short, rounded tubercles in two size classes. The mottled coloration of this nudibranch probably aids camouflage. The colours include yellow, brown, pink, green and white. There is also a bright red variety known as *Archidoris pseudoargus* var. *flammea*. Some of the large individuals may grow to 120 mm in length. The spawn is a broad ribbon laid in a spiral attached by one edge.

ECOLOGY Usually found on the low shore underneath large boulders. It feeds on the 'breadcrumb' sponge *Halichondria panicea* and on other sponges such as *H. bowerbanki* and *Suberites ficus* in the sublittoral.

DISTRIBUTION Common around Britain and Ireland and from Iceland to the Mediterranean.

SIMILAR SPECIES The species most likely to be confused with *Archidoris pseudoargus* is *Geitodoris planata* (p. 108) which differs in having stellate spots on the dorsum and brown specks on the underside of the mantle.

KEY CHARACTERISTICS Mottled pattern on mantle, colour variable. Mantle tubercles of two sizes.

Adult amongst jewel anemones *Corynactis viridis*, Cornwall, England.

Studio shot of adult, Gulen, Norway.

Two spawn coils on bedrock, Rathlin Island, Northern Ireland.

Doris cf. *ocelligera* (Bergh, 1881)

Doris ocelligera was originally described from the Mediterranean Sea; DNA sequences from specimens from the west coast of Ireland indicate that this is a separate species which we are here referring to as *Doris* cf. *ocelligera*.

DESCRIPTION The body is cream to yellow in colour. The mantle is covered with roughened tubercles with a darker spot at the tip. These tubercles appear to trap silt, giving them a capped appearance in undisturbed individuals. The rhinophores are pale yellow and there are a pair of tubercles at the base. The gills are simple and unipinnate. Body length to 25 mm.

ECOLOGY Found amongst sponges on rocky reefs and shipwrecks. The diet is presumably a sponge but has not been observed.

DISTRIBUTION This species has been found on a number of occasions in County Galway, Ireland, Dorset and Cornwall since 2003. It was previously known from the French Atlantic coast and the Mediterranean, and records of *Doris verrucosa* from Britain and Ireland are probably all this species.

SIMILAR SPECIES *D. verrucosa* (p. 124) is similar in colour and has roughened tubercles on the mantle but has larger gills and taller tubercles.

KEY CHARACTERISTICS Yellow dorid with fully retractile gills and rhinophores. Large and small tubercles covering the back, each with a darker terminal spot.

Adult on silty bedrock with the sponge *Amphilectus fucorum*, Connemara, Ireland.

Studio shot of adult, Connemara, Ireland.

Two individuals mating and spiral of spawn, amongst sea anemones *Metridium senile*, Donegal, Ireland.

Doris sticta (Iredale & O'Donoghue, 1923)

DESCRIPTION This nudibranch is pale yellow in colour. There is a network of paler channels connecting the mantle tubercles, the tips of the tubercles may be dark brown to pale purple in colour. The largest specimen recorded was 45 mm in length.

ECOLOGY *Doris sticta* has been observed eating the sponge *Ciocalypta penicillus* but has also been found in sites where this sponge was not present, so may have a broader diet.

DISTRIBUTION This southern species has been found occasionally on the west coast of Ireland, Skomer Island, South Wales, Lundy Island, Bristol Channel and along the coasts of the English Channel and south to the Mediterranean.

SIMILAR SPECIES Body shape and gill cluster similar to *Doris verrucosa* (p. 124) but no other species in the northeast Atlantic has angular tubercles joined by ridges.

KEY CHARACTERISTICS Yellow with purple-tipped mantle tubercles. A network of channels that connect the tubercles.

Adult amongst sponges and jewel anemones, Sark, Channel Islands.

Two individuals feeding on the sponge *Ciocalypta penicillus*, Sark, Channel Islands.

Spawn coil, Sark, Channel Islands.

Doris verrucosa Linnaeus, 1758

DESCRIPTION The mantle of this species is covered with tall tubercles with an irregular surface. The colour of the body is usually pale to bright yellow and there are often 2 diffuse grey lines running from the rhinophores to the gill cluster. In some individuals the grey colour becomes predominant. The rhinophores are pale yellow and there are a pair of large tubercles at the base, which fold into the opening left when the rhinophores retract. The gill pinnae are simple and unipinnate and when expanded are longer than the body width. Body length to 70 mm. The spawn is a large, coiled, yellow ribbon with a fluted upper margin.

ECOLOGY Found on shore and in shallow water beneath rocks. Reported to feed on the sponges *Hymeniacidon perleve, Halichondria panicea* and other *Halichondria* species.

DISTRIBUTION This species is common on the shore in southern Brittany and is known from the French Atlantic coast and the western Mediterranean.

SIMILAR SPECIES *Doris* cf. *ocelligera* (p. 120) is similar but smaller with more compact gills and smaller tubercles with a dark tip.

KEY CHARACTERISTICS Yellow dorid with fully retractile gills and rhinophores. Large and small tubercles covering the back, each with a darker terminal spot.

Adult showing the large tubercles at the base of the rhinophores, Frontignan, France. (Pierre Corbrion)

Adult showing the large gills and large dorsal tubercles, Frontignan, France. (Pierre Corbrion)

Doris verrucosa spawn, Ille-et-Vilaine, Bretagne. (Pierre Corbrion)

Dendrodoris limbata (Cuvier, 1804)

DESCRIPTION This is a relatively large nudibranch with adults growing to 50–70 mm in length. The colour of the mantle can vary from mottled greenish black, orange or brown through to individuals that are completely black. The rhinophores and gills are also black but may have yellow tips. It has a wavy mantle margin with a conspicuous yellow rim. *Dendrodoris* species have no radula and feed on sponges by dissolving the sponge tissue and sucking it up.

ECOLOGY Usually found under stones or on open rock down to 40 m depth. It has been reported to feed on the sponge *Suberites domuncula*.

DISTRIBUTION Primarily a Mediterranean species but it has also been reported from Portugal, the north coast of France and Sark in the Channel Islands.

SIMILAR SPECIES There are two other *Dendrodoris* species in the northeast Atlantic, *Dendrodoris grandiflora* and *D. herytra*, which have not yet been found north of Portugal.

KEY CHARACTERISTICS The yellow rim on the edge of the mantle margin is characteristic for this species.

Large individual crawling on seabed, Sark, Channel Islands. (Sue Daly)

Frontal view of large individual, Sark, Channel Isles. (Sue Daly)

Spotted colour form with spawn, Etang du Thau, Mediterranean coast of France. (Manon Marco)

Armina loveni (Bergh, 1860)

DESCRIPTION *Armina loveni* is a flattened, leaf-like nudibranch growing to 40 mm in length. The mantle bears a series of longitudinal folds or grooves, with the 2 short stubby rhinophores in an indentation at the front. The foot forms a shield across the front of the head. At the junction of the foot and mantle a deep groove containing small gills runs along the sides of the body. The mantle is brick red to dirty brown in colour, with pale lines along the tops of the longitudinal ridges. The spawn consists of a pale pink thread, tightly coiled in three dimensions.

ECOLOGY This species is found crawling on the surface or burrowing in muddy sand, usually in company with sea pens *Virgularia mirabilis*, on which it feeds.

DISTRIBUTION Infrequently recorded, with recent records from Kenmare River, Galway Bay, Strangford Lough and near Oban. Other records indicate a distribution from Norway to the Atlantic coast of France.

SIMILAR SPECIES Currently no other species of *Armina* are known from Britain and Ireland, but other similar species occur worldwide.

KEY CHARACTERISTICS Flattened leaf-like body with longitudinal ridges. Short stubby rhinophores at front of mantle.

Adult on muddy sand, Loch Crinan, Scotland.

Studio shot of adult, Strangford Lough, Northern Ireland.

Adults with the sea pen *Virgularia mirabilis*, Sogn Fjord, Norway. (Erling Svensen)

Antiopella cristata (delle Chiaje, 1841)

DESCRIPTION A semi-transparent nudibranch with numerous swollen cerata, each with a thin dark thread of digestive gland running through the centre. The tips of the cerata are coloured with an iridescent bluish white pigment, and similar pigment patches are found on the back, between the cerata and in the head region. The rhinophores have lamellae set at an angle, giving the appearance of spiral grooves. Between them is a cockscomb-like structure called a caruncle which is unique to the family Janolidae. A large species, growing to at least 75 mm. The spawn consists of a white or pale pink string wound in a wavy circle pattern, usually on the food. The eggs are in packets with clear patches between them, giving a beaded appearance to the spawn.

ECOLOGY Found in shallow sublittoral conditions, especially on sheltered rockfaces. It feeds on erect bryozoans, especially *Bugula* species and *Bicellariella ciliata*.

DISTRIBUTION A common species in moderate depths around most of Britain and Ireland. Recorded from Norway to the Mediterranean.

SIMILAR SPECIES This is a very distinctive species.

KEY CHARACTERISTICS Caruncle between rhinophore bases. Cerata extend across the front of the body.

Adult on bedrock with bryozoan turf, Skomer, Wales.

Two individuals on the bryozoan *Bugulina flabellata*, Skomer, Wales.

Spawn coil on the brown seaweed *Dictyota dichotoma*, Isle of Man.

Janolus hyalinus (Alder & Hancock, 1854)

DESCRIPTION A well camouflaged, brown-coloured nudibranch. The cerata are numerous, with rough, spiny surfaces and tapering to terminal knobs. They extend across the front of the body. They fall off with the minimum of disturbance and may poison other nudibranchs in a collecting dish. The rhinophores are brown, with spiral grooves and a crest structure as in the previous species. The digestive gland in the cerata is dark brown, and does not extend to the tip. Grows up to 30 mm in length. The spawn is a wavy spiral thread, coiled round the food and with a beaded appearance.

ECOLOGY Found amongst the erect bryozoans *Scrupocellaria* species on exposed rockfaces. It has been found on buoy ropes and artifical habitats in sheltered conditions where it appears to feed on the invasive species *Tricellaria inopinata*.

DISTRIBUTION Recent records from St. Kilda and the Summer Isles, Lough Hyne, Lundy Island and Looe in Cornwall. A rarely recorded species, also reported from Norway, France, the Netherlands, Spain and the Mediterranean.

SIMILAR SPECIES The rare *Proctonotus mucroniferus* is similar in appearance but lacks the crest between the rhinophores. This may be an anomaly in the original description and the two species may be the same, as the cerata are identical.

KEY CHARACTERISTICS Pointed cerata with rough surfaces, extending across front of body. Caruncle between rhinophores.

Adult amongst bryozoans, St. Kilda, Scotland.

Studio shot of adult, Looe, Cornwall, England.

Spawn coil on the sea squirt *Ascidiella aspersa*, Lough Hyne, County Cork, Ireland.

Janolus sp. A

DESCRIPTION The body and cerata are very transparent. The cerata are bulbous with slightly spiny surfaces and taper to a long tubular tip which is often held at an angle to the ceras. There are white circular markings at the tips of the cerata and small brown spots beneath these rings. The digestive gland in the cerata is dark brown and does not extend to the tip. Grows up to 25 mm in length.

ECOLOGY Found amongst the erect bryozoan *Scrupocellaria scruposa* which appears to be the food.

DISTRIBUTION Found at St. Kilda, the north coast of Ireland, western Scotland and the south coast of England.

SIMILAR SPECIES Can be distinguished from *Janolus hyalinus* (p. 132) by the white markings and the brown spots at the tips of the cerata.

KEY CHARACTERISTICS Pointed cerata with rough surfaces, extending across front of body. Ring of white and brown spots at the tips of the cerata. Caruncle between rhinophores.

Adult, Skerries, Portrush, Northern Ireland.

Studio shot, St. Kilda, Scotland.

Adult, offshore from Magilligan Point, Northern Ireland.

Hero formosa (Lovén, 1841)

DESCRIPTION A peculiar-looking nudibranch with a single row of bushy, branched appendages down each side of the body and across the front of the head. It has large propodial tentacles at the front of the foot. The overall colour is pale pinkish brown with white spots scattered down the body and a white centreline along the back. The erect rhinophores are smooth and finger-like, with white tips. Up to 40 mm in length.

ECOLOGY This is a nocturnally active species, found in hydroid rich sites where it feeds on *Tubularia indivisa*. During daytime it is usually found hiding beneath shells or stones or in bedrock crevices.

DISTRIBUTION A scarce species in Britain and Ireland most recent records are from the west coast of Scotland, near Oban, with occasional records in the Irish Sea and Kenmare River in southwest Ireland. In Norway it can regularly be found in sites with *Tubularia indivisa* present. A specimen was recently found with the deepwater coral *Lophelia pertusa* from the continental slope of the Rockall Trough, indicating a considerable depth range.

SIMILAR SPECIES Only one other species of *Hero* is known, *Hero blanchardi* from the western Mediterranean (not included here).

KEY CHARACTERISTICS Branching ceratal processes along sides of body and across front. White centreline down middle of back.

Four individuals and the spawn coil hiding beneath a coralline encrusted rock, Gulen, Norway.

Adult at night, feeding on the hydroid *Tubularia indivisa*, Gulen, Norway.

Spawn on underside of a shell, Gulen, Norway.

Tritonia hombergii (Cuvier, 1803)

DESCRIPTION *Tritonia hombergii* is the largest of the British nudibranchs, with a maximum recorded body length of 200 mm. The colour varies from white to pinkish brown. The mantle bears many soft, arborescent processes at its edge that function as gills. The back is covered with rounded tubercles which exude an irritant compound. The rhinophores are branched at the tips and have basal sheaths, as in all Tritoniidae. There are many small processes on the oral veil. The spawn consists of an untidily wound white rope of eggs with a transparent membrane along one edge, attaching it to the substratum.

ECOLOGY *T. hombergii* is a sublittoral species in Britain and Ireland where it has been found at depths down to 80 m. As a juvenile it is well camouflaged on its prey, the soft coral *Alcyonium digitatum*, but larger individuals are darker in colour and hide in crevices or beneath overhangs.

DISTRIBUTION This species is frequent in Scotland and the Irish Sea but becomes scarce on the south coast of England. In northern Norway it is different in colour, with orange individuals with orange gills being the common colour form and laying bright pink spawn coils.

SIMILAR SPECIES Small individuals could be confused with *Duvaucelia plebeia* (p. 148).

KEY CHARACTERISTICS Many irregular sized gills arising from the mantle edge. Many processes fringing the oral veil. Rhinophores with sheaths and branched processes at the tips.

On the octocoral *Alcyonium digitatum*, Isle of Man.

Studio shot, Strangford Lough, Northern Ireland.

Pink spawn coil on rock, Rathlin O'Birne Island, Ireland.

Tritonia griegi

(Cuvier, 1803)

DESCRIPTION *Tritonia griegi* is a large species, with a maximum recorded body length of 70 mm. The body is translucent white with contrasting lilac gills. The back and sides are covered with rounded tubercles. The rhinophores are branched at the tips and have basal sheaths, as in all Tritoniidae. There are many small processes on the oral veil.

ECOLOGY *T. griegi* is a coldwater species found in deep water but as shallow as 25 m in Trondheim Fjord. It feeds on the gorgonian coral *Paramuricea placomus*.

DISTRIBUTION This species is found in Norway and in deep water (800–1000 m) in the Bay of Biscay.

SIMILAR SPECIES This is a very distinctive species with the combination of white body and lilac gills.

KEY CHARACTERISTICS Many stalked, branching gills arising from the mantle edge. Many processes fringing the oral veil. Rhinophores with sheaths and with typical tritoniid branching tips.

Large individual with *Paramuricea placomus* in the background, Trondheim Fjord, Norway. (Erling Svensen)

At the base of *Paramuricea placomus*, Trondheim Fjord, Norway. (Erling Svensen)

Adult and spawn on the sea fan *Paramuricea placomus*, Trondheim Fjord, Norway. (Erling Svensen)

Duvaucelia lineata (Alder & Hancock, 1848)

DESCRIPTION The body of *Duvaucelia lineata* is translucent white, but sometimes a pinkish hue is present. There are 2 white lines that run from the base of the rhinophores, down the back and unite at the base of the tail. The head bears 4 oral processes that are tipped with white pigment. There may be up to 6 pairs of arborescent gills on the back of the animal. Adults may reach 34 mm in length. The spawn consists of a coiled thin ribbon of eggs.

ECOLOGY The diet of this nudibranch is the small octocoral *Sarcodictyon catenatum*. It is usually found in silty conditions on rocky surfaces.

DISTRIBUTION *D. lineata* has a wide distribution around Britain and Ireland and from Trondheim Fjord, Norway to Brittany, but is rather localised in its occurrence. It is not uncommon around Skomer Island and Lundy.

SIMILAR SPECIES The tritoniid rhinophores and distinctive coloration make this an easy species to identify. *Duvaucelia* was previously synonymized with *Tritonia* until the revision by Korshunova & Martynov (2020).

KEY CHARACTERISTICS Two white lines run down the back. Four processes on the oral veil.

Feeding on the octocoral *Sarcodictyon roseum* (seen here as a pinkish red creeping stolon with the polyps retracted), Clifden, Ireland.

Studio shot, Skomer, Wales.

Spawn coil, Connemara, Ireland.

Duvaucelia manicata (Deshayes, 1853)

DESCRIPTION *Duvaucelia manicata* is a small nudibranch, with a maximum body length of 15 mm. In juveniles the body is white, with irregular black pigment spots which coalesce into purple or brown in adult individuals. The edges of the mantle bear paired, branched gills, 4 pairs in an 11 mm specimen. The rhinophores have sheaths and are branched at the tips. There are 3–4 pairs of long, slender oral tentacles.

ECOLOGY The diet in British waters is unknown, but it is reported as feeding on the alcyonacean *Cornularia cornucopiae* in the Mediterranean.

DISTRIBUTION This species is frequent in the Mediterranean and reported from the Atlantic coast of France, but only a few records exist for the south coast of England.

SIMILAR SPECIES Easily distinguished from *Duvaucelia plebeia* (p. 148) by the longer oral processes and its distinctive coloration.

KEY CHARACTERISTICS White or purple body with irregular, elongate, dark spots in juveniles. Six to eight processes on the oral veil.

Individual amongst red algae in shallow water, Torbay, England. (Tamsyn Mann)

Studio shot, Lundy Island, Bristol Channel, England.

Two individuals mating, Mediterranean coast of France. (Enric Madrenas)

Duvaucelia odhneri

J. Tardy, 1963

DESCRIPTION This animal is usually pale salmon pink or pure white and may grow to up to 34 mm. The head bears 6 oral processes. There are approximately 8 pairs of gills on the dorsum that closely resemble the feeding polyps of the sea fan *Eunicella verrucosa*. The rhinophores are similar to other *Duvaucelia* species, with smooth-edged sheaths and branched tips.

ECOLOGY *Duvaucelia odhneri* is extremely well camouflaged on its prey, the gorgonian coral *Eunicella verrucosa*. It is only on close inspection of the sea fan that the nudibranchs may be found. The spawn consists of a fine string of eggs coiled around the stem of the gorgonian.

DISTRIBUTION A southwestern distribution in Britain and Ireland; the northern limit of its distribution appears to be Rathlin O'Birne Island, County Donegal, Ireland. It is known to occur in northern Spain, where it feeds on *Leptogorgia sarmentosa* and is white with a grey hue over the back. In the Mediterranean Sea it is found as far east as Croatia and Montenegro, where the preferred food is *Eunicella singularis* as well as other *Eunicella* species and *Leptogorgia sarmentosa*.

SIMILAR SPECIES The long, narrow body and plain coloration distinguish this species from other *Duvaucelia* species.

KEY CHARACTERISTICS Slender body without markings. Six processes on the oral veil.

Salmon pink individual feeding on the sea fan *Eunicella verrucosa*, Isles of Scilly, England.

Studio shot of a white individual, Mullaghmore, Ireland.

Three spawn coils and a white adult on the sea fan *Eunicella verrucosa*, Mullaghmore, Ireland.

Duvaucelia plebeia (Johnston, 1828)

DESCRIPTION This inconspicuous nudibranch is pale yellow with extensive greenish brown mottling. Usually there are 2 patches of darker pigment behind the rhinophores. It has 6 finger-like processes on its oral veil and up to 6 pairs of arborescent lateral gills. Adults vary in length from approximately 16 to 30 mm.

ECOLOGY *Duvaucelia plebeia* feeds on the soft coral *Alcyonium digitatum* and is usually found hiding at the base of the colony or amongst bryozoan undergrowth nearby. The spawn is a string laid in a convoluted coil, usually on rock at the base of *Alcyonium* colonies.

DISTRIBUTION This species is frequent around Britain and Ireland. It reaches its northern limit at Norway and its southern limit at Portugal.

SIMILAR SPECIES *Duvaucelia plebeia* is similar in appearance to *Duvaucelia manicata* (p. 144) but not as slender as that species and much darker in colour. Small *Tritonia hombergii* (p. 138) can be confused with this species, but have a bilobed frontal veil with more processes.

KEY CHARACTERISTICS Pairs of lateral arborescent gills. Mottled greenish brown coloration. Six processes on the oral veil in adults.

On coralline encrusted rock with a small colony of the octocoral *Alcyonium digitatum* above, Gulen, Norway.

Studio shot of adult, Skomer Island, Wales.

Two spawn coils, Rathlin Island, Northern Ireland.

Lomanotus genei

Verany, 1846

DESCRIPTION The colour of the body may be translucent white through to red, but both forms usually have yellow-tipped processes that form a wavy frill at the mantle edge. The rim of the rhinophore sheaths is modified to form similar yellow-tipped processes. Adults usually grow to 60 mm; however, occasional specimens may reach 94 mm in length.

ECOLOGY *Lomanotus genei* normally feeds on the hydroid *Nemertesia ramosa* but can sometimes be found on *Nemertesia antennina*. It has been found at depths down to 90 m. The spawn is a string of eggs wound irregularly around the hydroid.

DISTRIBUTION This animal is distributed from southern Norway to the Mediterranean but is rather rare and sporadic in occurrence.

SIMILAR SPECIES The existence of various colour forms of this species in Britain and Ireland has caused confusion in the past, with this species sometimes being considered to be conspecific with *Lomanotus marmoratus* (p. 152). Occasional juvenile individuals have been observed by the present authors which lack the yellow pigment and have different shaped pallial processes and may be a separate species.

KEY CHARACTERISTICS The zigzag frill of ceratal processes on the dorsum. Yellow-tipped processes and white or red body.

Red individual and pink spawn on the hydroid *Nemertesia antennina*, Rathlin Island, Northern Ireland.

Studio shot of a red individual, Connemara, Ireland.

Pink and white spawn coils on the hydroid *Nemertesia antennina*, Connemara, Ireland.

Lomanotus marmoratus (Alder & Hancock, 1845)

DESCRIPTION The body of this nudibranch is translucent white and mottled with brown and white pigment. Pure white individuals may also be found. The cerata-like processes are arranged along the edge of the pallial rim; the tips of these processes are swollen, with mucronate tips. The adults may grow to a length of 34 mm. This species can swim by vigorously flexing the body.

ECOLOGY *Lomanotus marmoratus* is usually found feeding on the calyptoblastic hydroid *Nemertesia antennina*. The adults often hide at the base of the *Nemertesia* colony. The spawn is a semi-transparent string of eggs laid in a tight zigzag along the stem of the hydroid and is very distinctive.

DISTRIBUTION Records exist from around Britain and Ireland and south to the northern coast of Spain. This species is inconspicuous and probably under-recorded.

SIMILAR SPECIES Occasionally small individuals which are probably *Lomanotus genei* (p. 150) are found which are almost colourless, lacking yellow or red pigment; others are spotted with dark brown. Distinctions with *L. marmoratus* are not clear, but these could be distinct species.

KEY CHARACTERISTICS Swollen-tipped cerata arranged along the pallial rim. Body normally mottled with dark pigment, occasionally unpigmented.

Adult on the hydroid *Nemertesia antennina*, Strangford Lough, Northern Ireland.

Studio shot of adult, Strangford Lough, Northern Ireland.

Spawn coil on the hydroid *Nemertesia anteninna*, Strangford Lough, Northern Ireland.

Scyllaea pelagica

Linnaeus, 1758

DESCRIPTION This nudibranch is widespread in the central ocean basins, associated with drifting seaweed such as *Sargassum bacciferum*. It is green or brown in colour with scattered white patches. There are 2 pairs of lateral lobes, which are flattened and bear small branching gills on their upper sides. The large rhinophore sheaths surround lamellate rhinophores and have a flap on their posterior surfaces. The whole body is irregular in outline, providing good camouflage amongst floating *Sargassum*. The animal can swim upwards by flexing its body vigorously, an important ability for a nudibranch which drifts about the oceans.

ECOLOGY This species feeds on tiny hydroids growing on the *Sargassum* seaweed with which it is associated.

DISTRIBUTION *Scyllaea pelagica* is a vagrant species, belonging in the Sargasso region off the Caribbean Sea. There appear to be no recent records, but it could turn up stranded on any western coast after gales in the Atlantic.

SIMILAR SPECIES There is no similar nudibranch in the Atlantic Ocean.

KEY CHARACTERISTICS Four flattened ceratal growths on the sides of the body. Green or brown colour with white patches.

Pair mating, amongst rafts of floating *Sargassum* seaweed, Papua New Guinea. (Norbert Wu)

Glaucus atlanticus

Forster, 1777

DESCRIPTION An aeolid nudibranch related to *Facelina*. Its shape is highly modified for floating at the surface of the sea. There are 3 clusters of cerata on each side of the body, with the first 2 being mounted on stalk-like projections of the sides of the body. The colour is blue with countershading, so the underside is very pale and the upperside dark. The cerata have cnidosacs which contain stinging cells from its food and can sting a human.

ECOLOGY *Glaucus atlanticus* floats at the surface of the ocean and feeds on siphonophores, a group related to the hydroids, which float freely at the surface of the sea. This group contains *Physalia physalis*, *Porpita porpita* and the *Velella velella*.

DISTRIBUTION These nudibranchs live in the areas of the ocean known as ocean gyres, places where the spinning of the planet causes the ocean water to rotate. This rotation enables a floating community of plants such as *Sargassum* and animals such as *P. physalis* and *P. porpita* to survive without being washed to a shore. *Glaucus atlanticus* has been found in the Canary Islands and the Azores, but not yet in mainland Europe, but its food washes up on western shores and it will probably be found.

SIMILAR SPECIES There are four species of *Glaucilla* which resemble *G. atlanticus* and have the same lifestyle. They are only found in the Indian and Pacific Oceans. *G. atlanticus* is larger and is found worldwide.

KEY CHARACTERISTICS Body with 3 ceratal clusters on each side. First 2 ceratal clusters are on long stalks. Unusual blue coloration.

Feeding on *Porpita porpita*, Tenerife, Canary Islands. (Sergio Hanquet)

Hancockia uncinata (Hesse, 1872)

DESCRIPTION The body of this rare nudibranch is pale green or pink with scattered white spots. There are up to 9 pairs of hand-shaped ceratal processes. The rhinophores are unusual in that their tips are swollen, and they have longitudinal lamellae. The oral veil is extended into 2 lateral flaps each with 3–4 finger-like projections. Adult specimens may reach 14 mm in length. The spawn is similar to *Doto* species, a flat ribbon laid in a concertina fashion, with a distinctive blue-white colour.

ECOLOGY Feeds on the tiny hydroid *Clytia hemisphaerica* which grows over other hydroids or on algae.

DISTRIBUTION Most of the records are from the Bay of Biscay; however it has been recorded from the Mediterranean coast of France, Spain and Naples in Italy, with scattered records as far north as southwest Scotland. It has also been recently recorded in southern Norway.

SIMILAR SPECIES Most likely to be mistaken for a *Doto* species (pp. 170–202), but the cerata are shaped like a curled hand and the rhinophores are distinctive.

KEY CHARACTERISTICS Small hand-like ceratal processes. Swollen-tipped rhinophores with sheaths and longitudinal lamellae.

Adult on kelp with hydroids, Egersund, Norway. (Erling Svensen)

Studio shot, Connemara, Ireland.

Spawn coil on *Dictyota dichotoma*, Connemara, Ireland.

Embletonia pulchra (Alder & Hancock, 1844)

DESCRIPTION The ground colour of this nudibranch is translucent white. Each ceras contains orange-brown lobes of digestive gland that are visible through the epidermis. There may be up to 7 pairs of club-shaped cerata on the sides of the dorsum. There is an increase in the length of the cerata towards the posterior end of the animal. The head is heart-shaped, the rhinophores are smooth; oral and propodial tentacles are lacking. Adults grow to approximately 7 mm.

ECOLOGY Reported to feed on a variety of shallow water hydroids. This species was previously classified as an aeolid due to its possession of cnidosacs and unbranched cerata, but now that the aeolids are classed as three groups within the cladobranchs, the distinction between dendronotaceans, arminaceans and aeolids no longer exists. It is found beneath stones or amongst coarse gravel or sand.

DISTRIBUTION Found around Britain and Ireland and from Norway to the Mediterranean. Not often recorded due to its minute size.

SIMILAR SPECIES This tiny nudibranch has a very characteristic arrangement of the cerata.

KEY CHARACTERISTICS Unbranched cerata-like gills in pairs along the sides of the back. Head with rhinophores and lateral oral flaps but no oral tentacles.

Individual on underside of a stone, Greenends Gully, Eyemouth, Scotland. (Jim Anderson)

Studio shot, Strangford Lough, Northern Ireland.

A tiny individual and also a chiton, on the underside of a stone, Strangford Lough, Northern Ireland. (Jon Chamberlain)

Dendronotus frondosus (Ascanius, 1774)

DESCRIPTION This nudibranch is variable in colour and has recently been separated from several other species. Individuals are grey-brown mottled with yellow, red or brown pigment. A distinctive character is the presence of compound tubercles on the back of the body. There are typically 6 pairs of gills along the pallial rim. The gills, oral veil and rhinophore sheaths are extended to form branched processes. Adults may grow to 40 mm in length.

ECOLOGY *Dendronotus frondosus* feeds on a variety of hydroids including *Sertularella*, *Halecium* and *Sertularia* species.

DISTRIBUTION *D. frondosus* can be found around Britain and Ireland. The species range extends southwards to the Atlantic coast of France; westwards to Canada, the United States, and the Pacific coast of Canada; and northwards into the Arctic Circle.

SIMILAR SPECIES Very similar to *Dendronotus lacteus* (p. 166) and *D. europaeus* (p. 162) with which it has been confused.

KEY CHARACTERISTICS Large arborescent gills arising from the mantle edge. Arborescent processes on the edge of the rhinophore sheaths. Rugose pyramidal tubercles on the sides of the body.

On hydroid, Gulen, Norway.

Studio shot, Portrush, Northern Ireland.

Spawn coil on the seaweed *Halidrys siliquosa*, Gulen, Norway.

Dendronotus europaeus

Korshunova, Martynov, Bakken & Picton, 2017

DESCRIPTION This nudibranch is variable in colour including predominantly white, yellow, red or brown individuals. The 7 pairs of gills are widely separated and frequently there is a rectangular brown patch between their bases. The gills and oral veil carry elongate branched processes. The edge of the rhinophore sheaths also carry long branched processes, usually with the posterior one longer than the others. Adults are typically 70–100 mm in length.

ECOLOGY *Dendronotus europaeus* feeds on the hydroid *Tubularia indivisa*.

DISTRIBUTION *D. europaeus* can be found around Britain and Ireland. The species range extends to southern Norway.

SIMILAR SPECIES *Dendronotus* species (pp. 160–168) are difficult to distinguish and have multiple colour varieties. This species has more finely and densely branched gills than the other species (Korshunova *et al.*, 2017b).

KEY CHARACTERISTICS Large arborescent gills arising from the mantle edge. Arborescent processes on the edge of the rhinophore sheaths with the posterior process elongated.

Adult amongst the eaten stems of the hydroid *Tubularia indivisa*, The Maidens, Northern Ireland.

Adult of the white colour form on the hydroid *Tubularia indivisa*, Shamrock Pinnacle, Northern Ireland.

Spawn coil on the hydroid *Tubularia indivisa*, Gulen, Norway.

Dendronotus sp. A

DESCRIPTION This is one of the more brightly coloured *Dendronotus* species, with bright yellow or white tips to the cerata. The body colour is translucent white with diffuse brown spots on the sides of the foot which sometimes coalesce into irregular brown patches. The digestive gland is clearly visible in the branches of the gills and is a similar shade of brown. The tips of the gills, rhinophore sheath papillae and oral veil papillae are tipped with bright cream or yellow. There are typically 7 pairs of gills along the pallial rim with the first 5 being large and the last pair very small or absent. There are pointed tubercles on the back and sides of the body which are brightly pigmented in cream or yellow. Adults may grow to 60 mm in length.

ECOLOGY *Dendronotus* sp. A feeds on the hydroid *Hydrallmania falcata*. It can be found mixed with *Dendronotus frondosus* in hydroid-rich sites exposed to strong tidal streams.

DISTRIBUTION Currently known from Northern Ireland and Norway.

SIMILAR SPECIES *Dendronotus* species (pp. 160–168) are difficult to distinguish and have multiple colour varieties. This species has a translucent white body marked with brown. Larger individuals have yellow spots which make it quite distinctive.

KEY CHARACTERISTICS Large arborescent gills arising from the mantle edge. Pointed yellow pustules on the back.

Adult amongst hydroids, Portrush, Northern Ireland.

Studio shot, Portrush, Northern Ireland.

Studio shot of spawn on the hydroid *Hydrallmania falcata*, Glenarm, Northern Ireland.

Dendronotus lacteus Thompson, 1840

DESCRIPTION This nudibranch is variable in colour with translucent white variants and red-brown or dark brown variants. Many individuals have a broken opaque white line along the middle of the back which expands into white diamonds between the gill pairs. There are typically 7 pairs of gills along the pallial rim with the first 4 being large and the last pair very small or absent. The oral veil and rhinophore sheaths are extended to form fairly short branched processes. Adults may grow to 120 mm in length.

ECOLOGY *Dendronotus lacteus* feeds on several hydroids. Juveniles usually feed on *Obelia* species, especially *Obelia geniculata* on kelp in sites exposed to strong tidal streams, while the adults are commonly found eating *Ectopleura larynx*.

DISTRIBUTION *Dendronotus lacteus* is apparently a northern species in northwest Europe. The species range extends from the Irish Sea through western Scotland northwards through Norway into the Arctic Circle.

SIMILAR SPECIES *Dendronotus* species (pp. 160–168) are difficult to distinguish and have multiple colour varieties. This species has shorter extensions on the rhinophore sheaths and more opaque white pigment on the back than the other species. Translucent white individuals are frequent in Norwegian populations (Ekimova *et al.*, 2015).

KEY CHARACTERISTICS Large arborescent gills arising from the mantle edge. Short arborescent processes on the edge of the rhinophore sheaths. Lozenge-shaped opaque white markings along the middle of the back. White individuals often have many small scattered red markings.

On kelp with the hydroid *Obelia geniculata*, Scarba, Scotland.

Studio shot, Garvellachs, Scotland.

Tangled spawn amongst stems of the hydroid *Ectopleura larynx*, Bodø, Norway.

Dendronotus yrjargul

Korshunova, Bakken, Grøtan, K. B. Johnson, Lundin & Martynov, 2020

DESCRIPTION This is one of the more brightly coloured *Dendronotus* species, with bright yellow tips to the cerata. The body colour is translucent white, and a pair of brown lines run longitudinally from between the rhinophores and gills, finishing before the tail. Between these lines are a series of raised pustules which are also bright yellow. Similar raised yellow pustules occur on the gill stalks, the sides of the body and the rhinophore sheaths. There are typically 7 pairs of gills along the pallial rim with the first 5 being large and the last pair very small or absent. The oral veil and rhinophore sheaths are extended to form long branched processes. Adults may grow to 90 mm in length. (Korshunova *et al.*, 2020a).

ECOLOGY *Dendronotus yrjargul* feeds on the hydroid *Abietinaria fusca*. Apparently confined to sites exposed to strong tidal streams, where the food is found.

DISTRIBUTION *D. yrjargul* is a northern species in northwest Europe. Currently only known from Trondheim Fjord in northern Norway.

SIMILAR SPECIES *Dendronotus* species (pp. 160–168) are difficult to distinguish and have multiple colour varieties. This species has 2 longitudinal brown lines and yellow spots which make it quite distinctive.

KEY CHARACTERISTICS Large arborescent gills arising from the mantle edge. Raised yellow pustules on the back, sides and bases of gills and rhinophore sheaths.

Adult on the hydroid *Abietinaria fusca*, Trondheim Fjord, Norway. (Erling Svensen)

Adult on the hydroid *Abietinaria fusca*, Trondheim Fjord, Norway. (Erling Svensen)

Adult and spawn on the hydroid *Abietinaria fusca*, Trondheim Fjord, Norway. (Viktor Grøtan)

Doto coronata (Gmelin, 1791)

DESCRIPTION The nudibranchs called by this name are probably an aggregate species consisting of *Doto* species which share the characteristics of red pigment spots on the tips of the ceratal tubercles and red pigment in the pseudobranch region on the inner face of each ceras. There are red to maroon pigment spots or streaks on the body. The smooth rhinophores have sheaths with dilated margins. The body is translucent white. Typically about 10 mm in length. The spawn consists of a ribbon which is laid in a concertina fashion.

ECOLOGY Individuals of this complex have been taken on a variety of hydroids.

DISTRIBUTION A common species recorded from around Britain and Ireland. The type locality is on the Dutch coast, and a neotype has been designated which was feeding on *Sertularia argentea* or *Sertularia cupressina*. Specimens on *Obelia* species are indistinguishable on DNA barcodes.

SIMILAR SPECIES *Doto hydrallmaniae* (p. 184) and *Doto sarsiae* (p. 200) have been separated from this complex by electrophoretic methods. It is likely that other morphs are also sibling species.

KEY CHARACTERISTICS Translucent white body with red or maroon pigment streaks. Cerata with spots of red pigment at the tip of each tubercle, and red areas on their inner faces.

On the hydroid *Obelia geniculata*, Gulen, Norway.

Studio shot of adult, Zeeland, Netherlands.

Adult and spawn coils amongst the hydroid *Obelia geniculata* on a kelp frond, Skomer, Wales.

Doto cuspidata

Alder & Hancock, 1862

DESCRIPTION A drab, dark-coloured nudibranch with no terminal spots on the ceratal tubercles. The rhinophore sheaths are slightly scalloped at the margins. The body is creamy white but obscured by streaks of brown or black pigment. There is a paler concentration of white glands in the tubercles of the cerata, and brown or black mottled pigment all over the ceratal surfaces. A large *Doto* species, reaching 25 mm in length. The spawn is a loose concertina of yellow ribbon, turning white as it develops.

ECOLOGY Seems to feed exclusively on *Nemertesia ramosa*, normally hiding near the base of the hydroid.

DISTRIBUTION Found as far south as Lundy in the Bristol Channel but more common in the northern part of Britain and Ireland. Frequent in Strangford Lough and the Irish Sea. In Norway a species resembling *Doto fragilis* is apparently recorded as this species because it has scalloped rhinophore sheaths.

SIMILAR SPECIES Similar in shape to *Doto pinnatifida* (p. 198) but immediately distinguishable by the lack of round pigment spots on the cerata.

KEY CHARACTERISTICS Body heavily marked with dark brown or black pigment. Pale glands in the tips of the ceratal tubercles.

Studio shot, adult and spawn on the hydroid *Nemertesia ramosa*, Strangford Lough, Northern Ireland.

Studio shot of adult, Rathlin Island, Northern Ireland. (Fred Pleijel)

Studio shot of spawn, Skomer Island, Wales.

Doto dunnei

Lemche, 1976

DESCRIPTION The body of this nudibranch is translucent white with red or black pigment streaks in dense patches on the back and sides. The cerata have round spots of black or red pigment at the tips of the tubercles, with irregular spots of pigment scattered over the surface between the tubercles. The rhinophores have sheaths with margins dilated and extended at the front. Grows to about 20 mm in length. The spawn is a long concertina of white ribbon.

ECOLOGY This species feeds exclusively on the hydroid *Kirchenpaueria pinnata* and is usually abundant on *Kirchenpaueria* clumps in late spring.

DISTRIBUTION This species has been reported from numerous localities on the western seaboard of Britain and Ireland, from Shetland, Norway, the Faroes south to the English Channel. It also occurs in the Galicia region of Spain and the Mediterranean Sea.

SIMILAR SPECIES *Doto millbayana* (p. 194) is very similar to *Doto dunnei*, but other red or black spotted *Doto* from the *Doto coronata* group do not have spots on the surfaces of the cerata except at the top of each tubercle.

KEY CHARACTERISTICS White body with red or black streaks of pigment. Multiple spots on surfaces of cerata in addition to terminal spots on tubercles.

Adult and spawn on the hydroid *Kirchenpaueria pinnata*, Isle of Man.

Studio shot of adult, Isle of Man.

Spawn ribbon on the hydroid *Kirchenpaueria pinnata*, Isle of Man.

Doto eireana

Lemche, 1976

DESCRIPTION This nudibranch is translucent white in colour with maroon-red spots on the tips of the ceratal tubercles and maroon pigment spots on the body. The cerata are bulbous, with few rows of blunt tubercles, becoming widest just below the tip. The spawn is a white ribbon laid in concertina fashion.

ECOLOGY *Doto eireana* is found exclusively on the hydroid *Amphisbetia operculata*, which is found in places with strong water movement, usually in the infralittoral zone. *Amphisbetia* frequently grows on stipes of the kelp *Laminaria hyperborea* and on steep rockfaces exposed to wave action.

DISTRIBUTION Records of this species are few, mainly because of its recent separation from *Doto coronata*, but it has been reliably reported from the west coast of Ireland and southwest England.

SIMILAR SPECIES This is very similar to *Doto hydrallmaniae* (p. 184) and can only be identified by consideration of the hydroid it is feeding on.

KEY CHARACTERISTICS White body with maroon spots on ceratal tubercles and body. Feeding on *Amphisbetia operculata*.

Studio shot, on the hydroid *Amphisbetia operculata*, Skomer, Wales.

Studio shot, Skomer, Wales.

Studio shot of spawn coil on the hydroid *Amphisbetia operculata*, Skomer, Wales.

Doto floridicola

Simroth, 1888

DESCRIPTION This *Doto* species is translucent white with extensive red pigment. There are red patches along the back and sides, extending to the front of the head. It has large red spots covering the ceratal tubercles, leaving narrow gaps between. It grows to 10 mm in length. The intensity of the red pigment is variable, from pink to red, but the edges of the pigment patches are slightly darker than the patch.

ECOLOGY *Doto floridicola* feeds exclusively on the hydroid *Aglaophenia kirchenpaueri*, which is found on rocky offshore reefs in the circalittoral zone.

DISTRIBUTION This species is confined to the southwest of Britain and Ireland, as far north as Skomer Island in Pembrokeshire and the Aran Islands in Galway Bay. It is found on the Atlantic coasts of France, Spain and Portugal and in the Mediterranean Sea.

SIMILAR SPECIES This species is more brightly coloured than *Doto lemchei* (p. 190), which it most closely resembles in shape.

KEY CHARACTERISTICS Red patches covering the ceratal tubercles which almost meet. White line on the rear side of the rhinophores.

Adult and spawn on the hydroid *Aglaophenia kirchenpaueri*, Skomer, Wales.

Studio shot, Skomer, Wales.

Numerous spawn coils on the hydroid *Aglaophenia kirchenpaueri*, Donegal, Ireland.

Doto fragilis

(Forbes, 1838)

DESCRIPTION This pinkish brown *Doto* has many large tuberculate cerata in 2 rows along the sides of the body. The cerata have numerous white glands in the tubercles and are slightly pointed. The rhinophore sheaths are trumpet-shaped with flared outer rims.

ECOLOGY This is a common species feeding on *Halecium halecinum*.

DISTRIBUTION Common around Britain and Ireland, and from Norway to the Mediterranean.

SIMILAR SPECIES Two other scarcer species are similar to *Doto fragilis* in having a brown hue and lacking dark spots on the tubercles. They are *Doto hystrix* (p. 186) and *D. lemchei* (p. 190). The common species found on *Nemertesia antennina* and *N. ramosa* is the subject of investigation at present but is distinct from this species by DNA and subtle features. It is called *Doto* cf. *fragilis* (p. 182) in this guide.

KEY CHARACTERISTICS Brown hue in skin but no dark surface pigment spots. White glands along the flanks of the body.

On the hydroid *Halecium halecinum*, Skomer, Wales.

Studio shot of adult, Gulen, Norway.

Studio shot of spawn coil on the hydroid *Halecium halecinum*, Skomer, Wales.

Doto cf. *fragilis*

DESCRIPTION This is a pale brown *Doto* with many large tuberculate cerata in 2 rows along the sides of the body. There are raised, white, glandular spots along the sides of the body. The rhinophore sheaths are trumpet-shaped with flared outer rims.

ECOLOGY This is a common species, especially in late summer, feeding on *Nemertesia antennina* and *N. ramosa* colonies. A giant form feeding on *Halecium muricatum* may be a distinct species.

DISTRIBUTION Common around Britain and Ireland, and from Norway to the Mediterranean.

SIMILAR SPECIES The name *Doto fragilis* (p. 180) should now only be used for animals feeding on *Halecium halecinum*; and this complex requires further study.

KEY CHARACTERISTICS Brown hue in skin but no dark surface pigment spots. White glands along the flanks of the body.

Two adults on the hydroid *Nemertesia ramosa*, Connemara, Ireland.

Studio shot, Skomer, Wales.

Adult and spawn on the hydroid *Nemertesia ramosa*, Skomer, Wales.

Doto hydrallmaniae

Morrow, Thorpe & Picton, 1992

DESCRIPTION A small *Doto* nudibranch, with dark red pigment spots on the cerata and with many subcutaneous white glands in the tips of the tubercles. The body and cerata are white, with scattered, elongate, ill-defined pigment spots on the body. There is a conspicuous circular area clear of pigment around the bases of the cerata. The digestive gland in the cerata is grey brown in colour.

ECOLOGY *Doto hydrallmaniae* feeds on *Hydrallmania falcata*, a hydroid found mostly on rock surfaces, stones, and pebbles in the circalittoral zone, especially in areas subject to scour from mobile sand or gravel. The animals live and lay narrow, tightly coiled concertinas of eggs on the stems of the hydroid.

DISTRIBUTION Recorded from scattered sites around the coasts of Britain and Ireland and one site in Denmark.

SIMILAR SPECIES Almost impossible to distinguish from *Doto coronata* (p. 170), *Doto eireana* (p. 176) and some other red spotted *Doto* species. The spawn coils are often more distinctive than the animals.

KEY CHARACTERISTICS Large, dark red pigment spots on the tubercles. Dark red marks on the inner faces of the cerata.

Adult and spawn on the hydroid *Hydrallmania falcata*, Isle of Man.

Studio shot, Galway, Ireland.

Spawn on the hydroid *Hydrallmania falcata*, Isle of Man.

Doto hystrix

Picton & Brown, 1981

DESCRIPTION This nudibranch is a spiky *Doto* species, similar in colour to *Doto fragilis* but with ceratal tubercles conical in shape, tapering to a sharp point. The rhinophore sheaths are characteristic, the rim being drawn out into a series of points.

ECOLOGY This is a scarce species, found feeding on the plumulariid hydroid *Schizotricha frutescens*, in deep water, usually below 25 m. This hydroid is usually found on rock, in moderate to strong tidal streams in clear oceanic water. The spawn is a typical *Doto* concertina, laid on the stem of the hydroid; it is often pale pink in colour.

DISTRIBUTION Widespread in Britain and Ireland but rather local in its occurrence. Also recorded from several sites in Norway.

SIMILAR SPECIES The sharply pointed tubercles on the cerata and the processes on the edge of the rhinophore sheath distinguish this from other species in the *Doto fragilis* (p. 180) colour group.

KEY CHARACTERISTICS Cerata without spots, with long, pointed tubercles. Rim of rhinophore sheaths with series of points.

Adult on the hydroid *Schizotricha frutescens*, Rathlin Island, Northern Ireland.

Studio shot, The Garvellachs, Scotland.

Pink and white ribbons of spawn on the hydroid *Schizotricha frutescens*, Rathlin Island, Northern Ireland.

Doto koenneckeri

Lemche, 1976

DESCRIPTION The ground colour of this nudibranch is translucent white through to cream. The dark pigment spots on the cerata are comma-shaped, not round as in other species. The terminal tubercle is considerably longer than the other ceratal tubercles. The back and flanks of the animal are heavily streaked with brown pigment. There is an unpigmented stripe between the ceratal bases. The spawn is a short, folded ribbon.

ECOLOGY The food of this species is the plumulariid hydroid *Aglaophenia pluma* which is common in shallow water, often growing on the brown seaweed *Halidrys siliquosa*, but also on rock surfaces.

DISTRIBUTION Recorded from the western coasts of Britain and Ireland, Portugal, and the Mediterranean coast of France.

SIMILAR SPECIES DNA evidence suggests that this is a species complex in Europe.

KEY CHARACTERISTICS Elongate dark spots on ceratal tubercles. Brown body pigment with pale lateral stripe.

Studio shot of adult and spawn on the hydroid *Aglaophenia pluma*, Strangford Lough, Northern Ireland.

Studio shot of adult, Strangford Lough, Northern Ireland.

Spawn coil on the hydroid *Aglaophenia pluma*, Connemara, Ireland.

Doto lemchei

Ortea & Urgorri, 1978

DESCRIPTION A small *Doto* species with no pigment spots on the cerata, but white glands are visible in the tips of the tubercles. The body and cerata have a light fawn or brown hue, and there is pale brown mottling on the head and back.

ECOLOGY *Doto lemchei* is a specialised feeder on *Aglaophenia tubulifera*, a plumulariid hydroid found mostly on rock surfaces in the circalittoral zone. The animals hide at the base of the hydroids but lay conspicuous spawn coils high on the stems. The spawn coil is short compared with most other *Doto* species, consisting of only 2 or 3 pleats.

DISTRIBUTION Recorded from Galicia in northwest Spain, north to Rathlin Island in Northern Ireland. Fairly common at Skomer Island in Wales and at some other localities in southwest Britain.

SIMILAR SPECIES Possible confusion with *Doto fragilis* (p. 180) but can be distinguished by the presence of pale brown mottling on the back of the animal and by the shape of the cerata. *Doto floridicola* (p. 178) is closely related and similar in size and shape, but immediately recognisable by the big red patches on the cerata tubercles.

KEY CHARACTERISTICS Lack of pigment spots on the tubercles. Brown hue to skin and pale brown pigment on the head and body.

Adult and spawn on the hydroid *Aglaophenia tubulifera*, Skomer, Wales.

Studio shot of adult, Skomer, Wales.

Spawn coil on the hydroid *Aglaophenia tubulifera*, Connemara, Ireland.

Doto maculata

(Montagu, 1804)

DESCRIPTION A tiny, inconspicuous *Doto* species of the '*coronata*' group, with 4 or 5 pairs of cerata. The ceratal tubercles are rather elongate and have terminal maroon-red spots, except for the apical tubercle, which often lacks the spot. The body is white with sparse mottling of red pigment. Normally up to 8 mm in length.

ECOLOGY This nudibranch feeds exclusively on the small plumulariid hydroid *Halopteris catharina*. This hydroid grows in dense patches on rocks, wrecks and on *Ascidia mentula* mostly in the circalittoral zone. *Doto maculata* lives and lays its white ribbon of spawn at the base of the hydroid colony.

DISTRIBUTION Sparsely recorded from the western coasts of Britain and Ireland and the Irish Sea, but probably not as uncommon as records suggest. It is present in southern Norway and there is one record from the Atlantic coast of Spain.

SIMILAR SPECIES Can be distinguished from *Doto coronata* (p. 170) by the lack of red pigment on the inner faces of the cerata.

KEY CHARACTERISTICS Red pigment spots on ceratal tubercles and on body. Ceratal tubercles elongate, terminal tubercle frequently unspotted.

Adult and spawn ribbon on the hydroid *Halopteris catharina*, Gulen, Norway.

Studio shot of adult, Gulen, Norway.

Studio shot of spawn coil on the hydroid *Halopteris catharina*, Gulen, Norway.

Doto millbayana

Lemche, 1976

DESCRIPTION A small *Doto* species of the '*coronata*' group, with typically 6 pairs of cerata in adults. The ceratal tubercles have terminal, round, maroon-red spots and extra irregular red spots. The body is white with sparse mottling of red pigment. The rhinophore sheaths have white pigment on their margins.

ECOLOGY This animal feeds exclusively on the plumulariid hydroid *Plumularia setacea*. This hydroid grows on larger hydroids such as *Nemertesia antennina* and *N. ramosa*. A larger form of *P. setacea* also grows amongst sponges in rapids or strong currents and may also harbour *Doto millbayana*.

DISTRIBUTION Recorded from the western coasts of Britain and Ireland and the Irish Sea, southern Norway and Portugal.

SIMILAR SPECIES Can be distinguished from *Doto coronata* (p. 170) by the lack of red pigment on the inner faces of the cerata. Shares a DNA barcode with *Doto dunnei* (p. 174), while these two could be conspecific, but lays a much shorter spawn coil and has differently shaped cerata.

KEY CHARACTERISTICS Red pigment spots on and between ceratal tubercles and on body. Conspicuous white rim to rhinophore sheaths.

Adult and spawn on the hydroid *Plumularia setacea*, Skomer, Wales.

Studio shot, Strangford Lough, Northern Ireland.

Studio shot, adult and spawn coil on the hydroid *Plumularia setacea*, Strangford Lough, Northern Ireland.

Doto onusta

Hesse, 1872

DESCRIPTION A slender *Doto* species of the '*coronata*' group growing up to 11 mm in length. The body is translucent white with maroon-red mottling and spots. The digestive gland is pinkish brown, making the cerata appear brown. There are 6–8 pairs of cerata which arise from an area that is free of pigment. The cerata have up to 5 rows of tubercles; each tubercle has a conspicuous spot of red pigment at its tip. The veil of the head is developed into 2 lobes. The rhinophore sheaths have only a few spots of red pigment. The translucent rhinophores are slender with some white mottling along their length.

ECOLOGY Feeds on the hydroid *Dynamena pumila*, which grows on brown seaweeds such as *Fucus serratus* and *Ascophyllum nodosum* mostly in the intertidal zone.

DISTRIBUTION This is a rarely recorded species; recent records are from Donegal in northwest Ireland, Strangford Lough in Northern Ireland, the Isle of Skye on the west coast of Scotland and the north coast of Devon in southwest England.

SIMILAR SPECIES The '*coronata*' group of *Doto* species are notoriously difficult to differentiate and we often rely on the prey species to help with the identification.

KEY CHARACTERISTICS Feeds on the hydroid *Dynamena pumila*.

On the hydroid *Dynamena pumila* which is growing on a kelp frond, Strangford Lough, Northern Ireland.

Studio shot, Strangford Lough, Northern Ireland.

Spawn coil on the hydroid *Dynamena pumila*, Strangford Lough, Northern Ireland.

Doto pinnatifida (Montagu, 1804)

DESCRIPTION *Doto pinnatifida* is one of the largest species of the genus *Doto*, large individuals reaching 30 mm in length. It is characterised by black-tipped tubercles on the sides of the body and on the cerata. Occasionally there are a few of these tubercles on the dorsum. The rhinophore sheaths have a series of black spots around the edges.

ECOLOGY The sole prey of this animal is the hydroid *Nemertesia antennina*. The spawn is a long, pleated ribbon, laid on the stem of the hydroid.

DISTRIBUTION Widespread and common in Britain and Ireland. The species' range extends as far north as southern Scandinavia and south to northern Spain.

SIMILAR SPECIES The only other *Doto* species with tubercles on the body is *Doto tuberculata* (p. 202), a smaller animal with tubercles arranged in irregular rows across the back, between the cerata. DNA evidence shows that the nearest species is *Doto cuspidata* (p. 172), but it has no black spots on the ceratal tubercles.

KEY CHARACTERISTICS Black-tipped tubercles on the sides of the body. Black spots on the edge of the rhinophore sheaths.

Adult amongst red algae and hydroid *Nemertesia antennina*, Connemara, Ireland.

Studio shot, Skomer, Wales.

Two adults and spawn on the hydroid *Nemertesia antennina*, Skomer, Wales.

Doto sarsiae

Morrow, Thorpe & Picton, 1992

DESCRIPTION A small *Doto* species of the *coronata* group, with up to 7 pairs of cerata. The cerata are club-shaped, tapering quickly to a blunt terminal tubercle. The tubercles are typically in 5 rows and have large, round, red pigment spots. The body is white with dense mottling of dark red pigment. The digestive gland is bright pink red in colour.

ECOLOGY This animal feeds on the athecate hydroid *Coryne eximia*. This hydroid grows in dense masses on kelp stipes and on rock surfaces subject to strong tidal streams or wave action, mostly in the infralittoral zone and sublittoral fringe. *Doto sarsiae* is found amongst the stems of the hydroid where it also lays its white ribbons of spawn.

DISTRIBUTION Described from the Isle of Man in the Irish Sea, but probably not uncommon in suitable exposed habitats.

SIMILAR SPECIES Difficult to distinguish from other forms of *Doto coronata* (p. 170) but animals fitting this description feeding on *Coryne eximia* will probably be this species. Similar animals have been found on *Garveia nutans*.

KEY CHARACTERISTICS Large red pigment spots on ceratal tubercles and on body. Cerata club-shaped, with blunt terminal tubercle.

Adults and spawn on the hydroid *Coryne eximia*, Rathlin Island, Northern Ireland.

Studio shot of adult and spawn, Calf of Man, Isle of Man.

Adults and spawn amongst the hydroid *Coryne eximia*, Strangford Lough, Northern Ireland.

Doto tuberculata

Lemche, 1976

DESCRIPTION The body of this nudibranch may reach 20 mm in length. The ground colour is translucent with a yellow hue. There are typically 5 to 7 pairs of cerata in adult specimens. The ceratal tubercles have black terminal spots and there are similar tubercles on the body. These are arranged in transverse rows across the back and sides, between the cerata.

ECOLOGY Feeds exclusively on the sertulariid hydroid *Sertularella gayi*. This hydroid is found mostly at silty sites with some current, in depths below the kelp zone. The animals usually attach themselves to the mid-rib of the hydroid and spread their cerata laterally when disturbed, providing good camouflage. The shape of the spawn is unusual for a *Doto* species, consisting of a loop of wavy ribbon laid along a branch of the hydroid.

DISTRIBUTION Found mainly on western coasts of Britain and Ireland and the north coast of France.

SIMILAR SPECIES Could be confused with the much commoner *Doto pinnatifida* (p. 198) but is smaller and does not have spots around the rhinophore sheaths.

KEY CHARACTERISTICS Pale yellow animal with black-spotted tubercles. Raised black-tipped tubercles in rows across the back.

On the hydroid *Sertularella gayi*, Isle of Jura, Scotland.

Studio shot, Isle of Jura, Scotland.

Spawn ribbons on the hydroid *Sertularella gayi*, Isles of Scilly.

Borealea nobilis

(Verrill, 1880)

There was a major revision to the families, genera and species within the Coryphellidae and Flabellinidae (Korshunova *et al.*, 2017a).

DESCRIPTION The body is translucent white in colour with opaque white pigment on the upper surface of the outer part of the robust oral tentacles and coating the outer part of the long rugose rhinophores. The cerata are inflated, with a narrow, red or red-brown digestive gland, and have a broad band of white pigment almost reaching the tip, with scattered small spots below it. The cerata are arranged as one continuous group with no clear gap between the first group and the rest. Typically grows to about 60 mm in length.

ECOLOGY A northern species in rocky sites with moderate currents, from 15 m depth downwards eating the hydroids *Ectopleura* and *Eudendrium* species. The spawn consists of an irregular coiled white thread which is draped amongst the food.

DISTRIBUTION Frequent in northern Norway with one record from Mulroy Bay in County Donegal, Ireland. Possibly mistaken for *Fjordia browni* in Britain and Ireland.

SIMILAR SPECIES *Fjordia browni* (p. 216) can be very similar but has less inflated cerata, less rugose rhinophores and an obvious gap between the first ceratal groups and the rest of the cerata.

KEY CHARACTERISTICS Opaque white markings only on the tail and head processes. Broad white bands on the cerata. Rhinophores long and rugose, fawn coloured when contracted.

Adult on the hydroid *Ectopleura larynx*, Saltstraumen, Norway.

Fully grown individual on rocky seabed, Northern Fjord, Norway. (Erling Svensen)

Tangled spawn amongst stems of the hydroid *Ectopleura larynx*, Bodø, Norway.

Coryphella rufibranchialis G. Johnston, 1832

DESCRIPTION The body is translucent white in colour with opaque white pigment on the tips of the oral tentacles and in a broken line along the centre of the back which becomes continuous on the long tail. The cerata are numerous and arranged in clusters along the sides and back of the body, almost hiding the white centreline. They are filled with red or orange-red granular digestive gland. The cerata have a thin, sometimes incomplete, ring of white pigment below the tip. Typically, about 15–25 mm in length, but well-fed individuals may be larger. The spawn consists of a thread which is laid in a smooth spiral like a clock spring.

ECOLOGY A common species in early spring at shallow exposed sites and deeper water which is exposed to tidal streams. The normal adult food is the hydroid *Tubularia indivisa*, but several smaller hydroids are eaten by juvenile specimens.

DISTRIBUTION A northern species in Britain and Ireland, occurring round Scotland and in the Irish Sea south to the Isle of Man, but apparently absent from the western coasts of Ireland and England. Further distribution includes Norway and the Atlantic coast of America.

SIMILAR SPECIES This species has been compared with *Coryphella verrucosa* (p. 208) using DNA barcodes and is apparently identical. It differs in having long cerata with transparent tips instead of white caps. It also has a different distribution, occurring south to the Irish Sea, while *C. verrucosa* has only been found in Shetland in the UK. Both species occur together in Norway. *Fjordia browni* (p. 216) and *Carronella pellucida* (p. 226) have been confused with this species.

KEY CHARACTERISTICS Long tail with clear spots in white centreline. Thin white rings at the tips of the cerata.

Adult on the hydroid *Tubularia indivisa*, Strangford Lough, Northern Ireland.

Studio shot, Gulen, Norway.

Spawn coil at the base of hydroid *Tubularia indivisa*, Gulen, Norway.

Coryphella verrucosa (M Sars, 1829)

DESCRIPTION The body is translucent pink in colour with opaque white pigment on the upper surfaces of the oral tentacles and in a broken line along the centre of the back which becomes continuous on the long tail. The cerata are short and swollen and arranged in clusters along the sides and back of the body. The bottom half is filled with red digestive gland. The cerata have a large cap of white pigment covering the tip. Typically, about 25–40 mm in length. The spawn consists of a thread which is laid in a smooth spiral like a clock spring.

ECOLOGY Frequent in sheltered places in Norwegian fjords feeding on hydroids including *Tubularia indivisa*.

DISTRIBUTION A northern species recorded only from Shetland in the United Kingdom but common in southern Norway and Denmark.

SIMILAR SPECIES This species has been compared with *Coryphella rufibranchialis* (p. 206) using DNA barcodes and is apparently identical. It differs in having short cerata with white tips instead of white rings and thicker oral tentacles. It also has a different distribution, occurring south to Shetland in the UK, while *C. rufibranchialis* is frequent in the Irish Sea. Both species occur together in Norway, but with some habitat differences.

KEY CHARACTERISTICS Long tail with clear spots in white centreline. Broad white caps at the tips of the cerata.

Adult on coralline encrusted bedrock, Gulen, Norway.

Studio shot, Gulen, Norway.

Spawn coil on bryozoan encrusted rock, Gulen, Norway.

Gulenia borealis (Odhner, 1922)

DESCRIPTION The genus *Gulenia* contains species of coryphellids with a distinctive shape and arrangement of the cerata. The cerata are numerous and arranged along the sides of the body with no obvious grouping into clusters. In this species there is no opaque white pigment on the body or surfaces of the cerata apart from a thin ring just below the tip of the cerata. Typically, about 30 mm in length.

ECOLOGY A moderately deepwater species occasionally dredged in the North Sea in considerable numbers. Individuals have been found eating fallen sea pens, *Funiculina quadrangularis*.

DISTRIBUTION Found in fjords in Norway and Sweden and in the North Sea.

SIMILAR SPECIES Body shape and arrangement of the cerata are very similar to the other *Gulenia* species (pp. 212–214), but *G. borealis* has no white lines on the body or spots on the cerata.

KEY CHARACTERISTICS Coryphellid with fusiform cerata continuous down the sides of the body. No white lines on the body or white marks on the cerata apart from a subterminal thin ring.

Adult eating a small athecate hydroid, Idde Fjord, Norway/Sweden border. (Heine Jensen)

Studio shot, Idde Fjord, Norway/Sweden border. (Heine Jensen)

Three animals feeding on a fallen sea pen *Funiculina quadrangularis*, Gullmarn Fjord, Sweden. (Klas Malmgren)

Gulenia monicae

Korshunova, Martynov, Bakken, Evertsen, Fletcher, Mudianta, Saito, Lundin, Schrödl & Picton, 2017

DESCRIPTION The body is translucent white in colour with a broad line of opaque white pigment down the middle of the back and thick white lines on the sides. The cerata are numerous, slightly swollen and not in groups. The digestive gland is bright to dull red and half fills the cerata. There are normally white spots on the cerata and a thin ring of white pigment below the tip, but these may be almost absent. Typically, about 30 mm in length. The spawn consists of a very thin thread which is laid in an irregular spiral.

ECOLOGY Amongst hydroids in areas with moderate current. Found on bare rock and amongst the hydroids *Ectopleura larynx* and *Tubularia indivisa* but may also be feeding on smaller hydroids epizoic on *T. indivisa*.

DISTRIBUTION Found in southern Norway from the Sogn Fjord to Trondheim Fjord. May be more widespread.

SIMILAR SPECIES Extremely similar to *Gulenia orjani* (p. 214), but clearly different on DNA barcodes. *G. monicae* is longer and narrower in the body and slightly less pigmented in white, but some individuals may be indistinguishable.

KEY CHARACTERISTICS Broad white longitudinal lines down the back and sides of the body. Sparse white spots on the swollen cerata. Slim body and short cerata.

Adult feeding on a hydroid that is growing on the stem of the hydroid *Tubularia indivisa*, Gulen, Norway.

Studio shot, Gulen, Norway.

Tangled spawn amongst the hydroid *Tubularia indivisa*, Gulen, Norway.

Gulenia orjani

Korshunova, Martynov, Bakken, Evertsen, Fletcher, Mudianta, Saito, Lundin, Schrödl & Picton, 2017

DESCRIPTION The body is translucent white in colour with a broad line of opaque white pigment down the middle of the back and thick white lines on the sides. The cerata are numerous, slightly swollen and not in groups. The digestive gland is bright red or grey-black and half fills the cerata. There are white streaks and spots on the cerata and a thin ring of white pigment below the tip. Typically, about 30 mm in length. The spawn consists of a very thin thread which is laid in an irregular spiral.

ECOLOGY Amongst hydroids in areas with moderate current. Feeding on hydroid *Eudendrium* spp. and amongst *Ectopleura larynx* and *Tubularia indivisa*.

DISTRIBUTION Found in southern Norway from the Sogn Fjord to Trondheim Fjord. May be more widespread.

SIMILAR SPECIES Extremely similar to *Gulenia monicae* (p. 212), but clearly different on DNA barcodes. *G. orjani* is shorter and broader in the body and can have a lot of opaque white pigment on the body and cerata. These two species are frequently found together.

KEY CHARACTERISTICS Broad white longitudinal lines down the back and sides of the body. Numerous white streaks and spots on the swollen cerata. Broad body and moderately long cerata.

On the hydroid *Eudendrium islandicum*, Gulen, Norway.

Studio shot of adult, Gulen, Norway.

Adult and spawn on the hydroid *Eudendrium islandicum*, Gulen, Norway.

Fjordia browni (Picton, 1980)

DESCRIPTION The body is translucent white in colour with patches of opaque white pigment on the tips of the long, pointed oral tentacles, smooth rhinophores and tail. The cerata are filled with red or red-brown digestive gland and have a broad ring of white pigment below the tip. There are conspicuous pointed propodial tentacles at the front corners of the foot in all coryphellids. Typically, about 20–50 mm in length, but well-fed individuals may be larger. The spawn consists of a thread which is laid in a wavy spiral.

ECOLOGY A common species in spring and early summer in shallow exposed sites and deeper water which is exposed to tidal streams. The normal food is the hydroid *Tubularia indivisa,* but other hydroids are sometimes eaten, such as *Eudendrium* species and the solitary hydroid *Corymorpha nutans.*

DISTRIBUTION Found throughout Britain and Ireland, and as far north as Iceland. Recorded from the Atlantic coast of France, but confusion with other species makes new records valuable.

SIMILAR SPECIES Could be confused with *Coryphella rufibranchialis* (p. 206) but can be distinguished by the arrangement of the cerata and the white line that is present on the tail of *C. rufibranchialis* and absent in *F. browni*. Large individuals are very hard to distinguish from *Borealea nobilis* (p. 204) and small individuals look very like *Microchlamylla gracilis* (p. 222). *Carronella pellucida* (p. 226) shares the same coloration but has white caps, not rings, on the cerata.

KEY CHARACTERISTICS White markings only on the tips of the tail and head processes. Broad white rings on the cerata.

Two individuals on the hydroid *Tubularia indivisa*, Rathlin O'Birne Island, Ireland.

Studio shot, Gulen, Norway.

Spawn coil on the hydroid *Tubularia indivisa*, Gulen, Norway.

Fjordia chriskaugei

(Lovén, 1846)

DESCRIPTION The body is translucent white in colour with thin lines of opaque white pigment. The cerata are numerous and arranged in clusters along the sides of the body. They are filled with digestive gland of variable colour, red, red-brown or yellow-orange. There are a series of dashes of white pigment on the sides of the cerata and the cnidosacs are clearly visible with no opaque pigment ring covering them. Typically, about 20–50 mm in length, but well-fed individuals may be larger. The spawn consists of a thread which is laid in a wavy spiral.

ECOLOGY A common species in spring and early summer in shallow exposed sites and deeper water which is exposed to tidal streams. The normal food is the hydroid *Tubularia indivisa,* but other hydroids are sometimes eaten, such as *Corymorpha nutans.* Often found in mixed populations with *Fjordia browni.*

DISTRIBUTION Found from Norway southwards to the English Channel.

SIMILAR SPECIES Previously included within *Coryphella* (now *Fjordia*) *lineata*. DNA evidence suggests that it is the sister species to *Fjordia browni* (p. 216).

KEY CHARACTERISTICS White longitudinal lines down the back and sides of the body. White dashes on the cerata or cerata with no markings. Absence of opaque white pigment obscuring the cnidosacs.

Three adults and spawn on the hydroid *Tubularia indivisa*, Gulen, Norway.

Studio shot, Gulen, Norway.

Adult and spawn coil on the hydroid *Tubularia indivisa*, Gulen, Norway.

Fjordia lineata (Lovén, 1846)

DESCRIPTION The body is translucent white in colour with thin lines of opaque white pigment. The cerata are numerous and arranged in clusters along the sides of the body. They are filled with digestive gland of variable colour, red to almost black. There are 2 lines of white pigment on the sides of the cerata and the outer line expands into a ring of white pigment below the tip. Typically, about 20–40 mm in length, but well-fed individuals may be larger. The spawn consists of a thread which is laid in a wavy spiral.

ECOLOGY A common species in spring and early summer in shallow exposed sites and deeper water which is exposed to tidal streams. The normal food is the hydroids *Eudendrium* spp., *Ectopleura larynx* and *Bougainvillia*.

DISTRIBUTION Found from Norway southwards, throughout Britain and Ireland, and as far south as the Mediterranean Sea.

SIMILAR SPECIES *Fjordia chriskaugei* (p. 218) was until recently included in the range of variation believed to be the species *Coryphella lineata*. DNA evidence revealed several distinct and not closely related species, including two species of *Gulenia*, with essentially the same pattern of white lines along the centre of the back and sides. The fact that this pattern is also shared with *Hero formosa* and many other aeolids suggests that it may be an ancestral character.

KEY CHARACTERISTICS White longitudinal lines down the back and sides of the body. Opaque white lines on the cerata expanding into a ring which partly covers the cnidosac.

Adult on bedrock with coralline algae and didemnid ascidians, Lough Hyne, Ireland.

Studio shot of adult, Strangford Lough, Northern Ireland.

Adult and spawn amongst hydroids, Connemara, Ireland.

Microchlamylla gracilis (Alder & Hancock, 1844)

DESCRIPTION The cerata in this species are normally filled with red-coloured digestive gland, but green individuals (var. *smaragdina*) are found on occasion. The body is translucent white, with patches of white pigment at the tips of the rhinophores, oral tentacles and tail, and thin rings of white pigment at the tips of the cerata. The anus is beneath the gap between the second and third bunches of cerata. A small species, reaching 12–15 mm at maturity.

ECOLOGY Found mostly in semi-sheltered conditions where there is water movement from tidal streams. Feeds on *Eudendrium* species, especially *Eudendrium arbuscula* and *E. annulatum*, and is usually abundant when found. The spawn is a white string wound untidily amongst the food. When laid on a flat surface it forms a Greek-key type pattern.

DISTRIBUTION Found from western Scotland, Ireland, Wales and England. Further positive records include Iceland, Norway, Denmark, the Netherlands and the Atlantic coast of America. There are a few records from Brittany but none from further south.

SIMILAR SPECIES Easily confused with juveniles of other coryphellid species, especially *Fjordia browni* (p. 216), but the presence of internal opaque white globules of mature ovotestis in animals of 10–12 mm is a good identifying feature.

KEY CHARACTERISTICS Anus position between second and third ceratal clusters. Small size at maturity.

On the hydroid *Eudendrium* sp., Gulen, Norway.

Studio shot, Gulen, Norway.

Several individuals and their spawn on the hydroid *Eudendrium arbusculum*, Saltstraumen, Norway.

Edmundsella pedata (Montagu, 1815)

DESCRIPTION This nudibranch is easily recognised by the overall pink-purple coloration of the body and processes. Opaque white pigment is present on the extremities and as white rings at the tips of the cerata. The digestive gland is usually red in colour, partly masked by the purple hue. Typically, about 20 mm in length.

ECOLOGY Found usually in ones or twos in moderately exposed rocky sublittoral areas. The food is a sparsely branched, spindly species of *Eudendrium*, probably usually *Eudendrium ramosum*. The spawn is a thin white thread normally wound round the *Eudendrium* on which the animals are feeding.

DISTRIBUTION Common and widespread around Britain and Ireland, north to Norway and south to the Mediterranean Sea.

SIMILAR SPECIES Structurally similar to other flabellinids but distinguished by its purple hue. *Flabellina affinis* (not included here) shares this coloration but has lamellate rhinophores and more pedunculate cerata and is found in the Mediterranean Sea and Portugal, but not further north.

KEY CHARACTERISTICS Overall pink-purple coloration. Cerata in bunches and joined at their bases.

Three individuals on the hydroid *Eudendrium ramosum*, growing as an epiphyte on a kelp stipe, Gulen, Norway.

Studio shot, Donegal, Ireland.

Edmundsella pedata laying a spawn coil, Mediterranean coast of Spain. (Enric Madrenas)

Carronella pellucida (Alder & Hancock, 1843)

DESCRIPTION The body is translucent white in colour with opaque white pigment on the tips of the oral tentacles, rhinophores and tail. The cerata are filled with red digestive gland and are capped with white pigment extending right over the tips. Typically, about 30 mm in length when fully grown.

ECOLOGY An uncommon species breeding in early summer in sites which are sheltered from wave action but exposed to tidal streams. The normal food is the hydroid *Eudendrium arbuscula*, but other *Eudendrium* species may be eaten. The spawn consists of a thread which is laid in a wavy spiral coiled amongst the food and on nearby rocks.

DISTRIBUTION A northern species in Britain and Ireland, occurring around Scotland and in the Irish Sea. There is a single recent record confirmed by a specimen from Lough Hyne, County Cork. Further distribution includes Norway and the Atlantic coast of America.

SIMILAR SPECIES Possible confusion with *Coryphella rufibranchialis* (p. 206) and *Fjordia browni* (p. 216) but can be distinguished by the fact that the cerata arise from peduncles.

KEY CHARACTERISTICS Long cerata of fairly even size giving a shaggy appearance. White caps covering the tips of the cerata.

Feeding on the hydroid *Eudendrium arbusculum*, Gulen, Norway.

Studio shot, Gulen, Norway.

Spawn coil attached to the hydroid *Eudendrium arbusculum*, Gulen, Norway.

Tergipes tergipes (Forsskål, 1775)

DESCRIPTION A tiny aeolid with single cerata arranged alternately along the sides of the body. The body is translucent white with red markings on the sides of the head and just behind the rhinophore bases. The digestive gland is grey in colour and shows through the back as a branching vessel. The cerata are swollen in shape and have large white cnidosacs at the tips. The oral tentacles are short but the rhinophores are long and tapering. Only 6–8 mm in length when fully grown. The spawn consists of small white capsules.

ECOLOGY Feeds on several species of *Obelia* but especially *Obelia geniculata* (normally found on kelp fronds) and *Laomedea flexuosa*.

DISTRIBUTION This species has a widespread distribution, likely to have been moved around as part of a fouling community by boats and aquacultural activity. It is widespread and common throughout Britain, Ireland, Norway and the north coast of France but is also found in Portugal, the Mediterranean Sea, the Atlantic coast of the United States with one record from South Africa. It is frequently overlooked because of its small size.

SIMILAR SPECIES *Eubranchus exiguus* (p. 268) is often found with *Tergipes tergipes* and is equally small. It can easily be distinguished with a hand lens or low-power microscope by the more numerous cerata and dark rings on the rhinophores.

KEY CHARACTERISTICS Cerata single, not in rows, along each side of the body. Red streaks on the head.

Numerous individuals on the hydroid *Laomedea flexuosa*, Donegal, Ireland.

Studio shot of adult, Idde Fjord, Sweden. (Fredrik Pleijel)

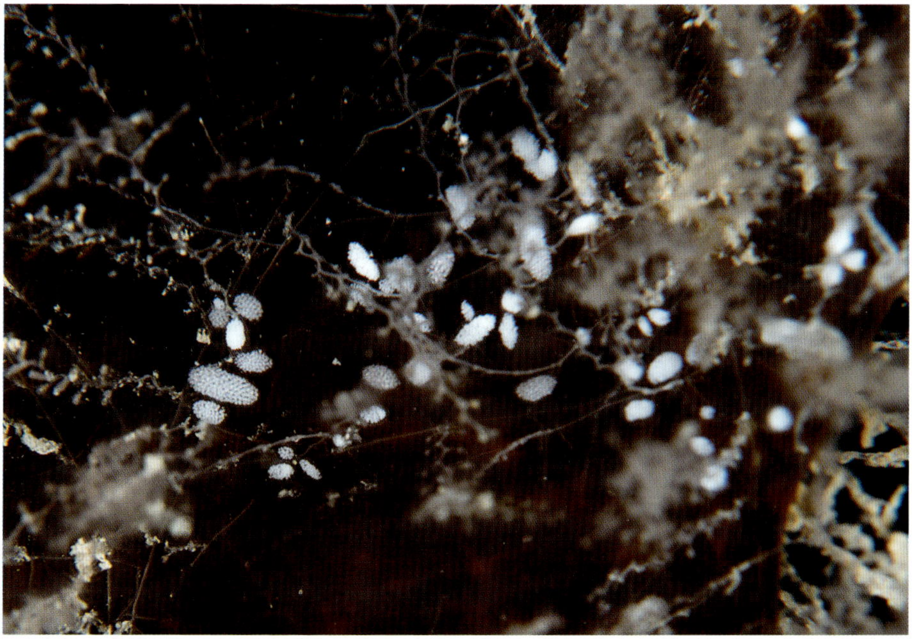

Oval spawn masses on the hydroid *Obelia geniculata* on kelp, Skomer, Wales.

Bohuslania matsmichaeli

Korshunova, Lundin, Malmberg, Picton & Martynov, 2018

DESCRIPTION A small aeolid with a translucent skin and no superficial pigment. The digestive gland may be visible in a zigzag pattern running down the broad back and branching out to the ceratal groups. The cerata are less numerous than in *Cuthona nana* and are positioned to the sides of the body in a way that is reminiscent of *Calma* species. The cnidosacs are small but white and conspicuous. Typically, 10 mm when adult.

ECOLOGY This species feeds on *Cordylophora caspia,* a brackish water athecate hydroid. Fine spirals of eggs are laid amongst the hydroids or on flat surfaces where the hydroids are attached.

DISTRIBUTION Found in the Idde Fjord on the border of Norway and Sweden in brackish water (Korshunova *et al.*, 2018).

SIMILAR SPECIES The other nudibranch likely to be found in brackish water is *Tenellia pallida* (p. 244).

KEY CHARACTERISTICS Small white cnidosacs and absence of body pigment. Unusual habitat, in brackish water.

Adult amongst hydroids, Idde Fjord, Sweden. (Mats Larsson)

Studio shot of fully grown individual, Idde Fjord, Sweden. (Fredrik Pleijel)

Animal with spawn coil, Idde Fjord, Sweden. (Mats Larsson)

Cuthona nana

(Alder & Hancock, 1842)

DESCRIPTION This small nudibranch is predominantly pink in colour, due to the orange-pink digestive gland in the many crowded cerata. The cerata and rhinophores have pale tips, and the body is translucent white. The cerata are more numerous than in trinchesiids and extend along the sides of the head, in front of the rhinophores. Individuals begin to spawn at about 12 mm but may grow to 28 mm in length.

ECOLOGY This species feeds on *Hydractinia echinata* which is a pink, athecate hydroid normally found on hermit crab shells in sheltered, muddy localities. Convoluted spirals of eggs are usually laid on the shell where the animals have been feeding.

DISTRIBUTION Found around Britain and Ireland, and elsewhere from Northern France, Scandinavia, Greenland and the Atlantic coast of North America.

SIMILAR SPECIES The coloration of *Catriona aurantia* (p. 236) is similar, and these species have been confused in the past.

KEY CHARACTERISTICS Numerous cerata with pink digestive gland. Small white tips to cerata due to white epidermal gland cells. Unusual habitat, on hermit crab shells with *Hydractinia*.

Studio shot of adult on the hydroid *Hydractinia echinata*, Strangford Lough, Northern Ireland.

Studio shot of adult, Strangford Lough, Northern Ireland.

Spawn mass with veligers about to hatch, Connemara, Ireland.

Cuthonella concinna (Alder & Hancock, 1843)

DESCRIPTION A rather drab nudibranch with grey digestive gland in the cerata and white pigment flecks on the ceratal surfaces, most concentrated at the tips of the cerata. The tips of the oral tentacles and rhinophores are also pigmented with white, but the rest of the body is translucent, with the opaque white ovotestis lobules showing through clearly in mature individuals. Typically, 10–12 mm in length when fully mature.

ECOLOGY This species feeds on the hydroid *Sertularia argentea* which is usually found in sites exposed to strong water movement from either tidal streams or wave action. The spawn is a thin white ribbon wound amongst the food.

DISTRIBUTION A northern species in Britain and Ireland, positively recorded from the northern part of the Irish Sea and western Scotland, with the most southerly records from Skomer Island, Pembrokeshire. Further distribution includes the Netherlands, Denmark, Sweden, Norway, Iceland and the Atlantic coast of America.

SIMILAR SPECIES Possible confusion with *Diaphoreolis viridis* (p. 238); however in *D. viridis* the digestive gland is dark green, and the body often has a faint yellow hue.

KEY CHARACTERISTICS Grey digestive gland in cerata. White pigment on cerata and head tentacles.

Two individuals on the hydroid *Sertularia argentea*, Isle of Man.

Adult on the hydroid *Sertularia argentea*, Strangford Lough, Northern Ireland.

Adult and spawn on the hydroid *Sertularia argentea*, Strangford Lough, Northern Ireland.

Catriona aurantia (Alder & Hancock, 1842)

DESCRIPTION The cerata of this nudibranch are more swollen than in other trinchesiids. The digestive gland is orange pink in colour and the tips of the cerata have a broad white band of tiny epidermal glands. In larger specimens the rhinophores develop a pale orange suffusion. The foot is broad and rounded anteriorly. Large individuals may exceed 20 mm in length. The spawn consists of curved, lozenge-shaped packets of eggs.

ECOLOGY Feeds on *Ectopleura larynx*. Individuals are usually found amongst the stems of the *Ectopleura* and are thought to feed by eating through the stems rather than grazing directly on the polyps. Usually found in exposed places, in strong tidal streams, and in shallow water.

DISTRIBUTION Found around Britain, Ireland, Norway, and south to the Bay of Biscay. This species was previously synonymised with *Catriona gymnota* but DNA studies have shown that this is a separate species found on the Atlantic coast of North America.

SIMILAR SPECIES Similar in coloration to *Cuthona nana* (p. 232) but with far fewer cerata and a different habitat.

KEY CHARACTERISTICS Orange-pink digestive gland. Unpigmented body. Tiny white epidermal glands form a white band around tips of cerata.

Adult feeding on the hydroid *Tubularia indivisa*, Gulen, Norway.

Studio shot of adult, Gulen, Norway.

Tangled spawn amongst the hydroid *Tubularia indivisa*, Isle of Man.

Diaphoreolis viridis (Forbes, 1840)

DESCRIPTION This trinchesiid is distinguished by its green ceratal contents and splashes of yellow-white pigment. The body is translucent white, often with a faint yellow hue. The cnidosacs at the tips of the cerata are large and conspicuous, off-white in colour. Streaks and spots of white pigment extend along the dorsal surfaces of the cerata. The brown jaws are clearly visible through the head in front of the rhinophores. Grows to about 15 mm in length.

ECOLOGY Feeds on the hydroids of the genus *Sertularella*, especially *Sertularella rugosa*. Found in shallow exposed and semi-sheltered rocky areas.

DISTRIBUTION Appears to be a northern species in northwest Europe. It is common in the north of Britain and Ireland, though records exist from the Atlantic coast of France. It has been recorded from all along the coasts of Norway. Specimens from Iceland may grow larger and develop more dense white pigmentation dorsally.

SIMILAR SPECIES *Trinchesia caerulea* (p. 246) and *Cuthonella concinna* (p. 234) are similar in anatomy, both internally and externally, but easily distinguished by coloration.

KEY CHARACTERISTICS Green ceratal contents. Yellow-white pigment on dorsal surfaces of cerata.

Adult on the hydroid *Sertularella* sp., Gulen, Norway.

Studio shot of adult, Gulen, Norway.

Studio shot of spawn, Gulen, Norway.

Rubramoena amoena (Alder & Hancock, 1845)

DESCRIPTION This inconspicuous nudibranch has a translucent body with patches of brown pigment at the bases of the cerata, and brown rings on the rhinophores and oral tentacles. The back of the body and the surfaces of the cerata are speckled with gold or yellowish white pigment flecks, with the densest speckling at the tips of the head tentacles and cerata. The jaws are visible in the transparent head, and the corners of the foot are rounded. Typically, about 10 mm in length.

ECOLOGY Found on the common hydroid *Halecium halecinum*, which seems to be the exclusive food. The spawn is a thin white scalloped ribbon, usually wound untidily around the food.

DISTRIBUTION Widespread throughout Britain and Ireland and known from as far north as Norway and as far south as the Mediterranean.

SIMILAR SPECIES *Rubramoena rubescens* (p. 242) is very similar to this species, but the brown coloration is replaced by red and the oral tentacles have no band but a white continuous upper surface instead.

KEY CHARACTERISTICS Brown rings on head tentacles and patches at the bases of the cerata. Gold specks on body, cerata and head tentacles.

Adult on the hydroid *Halecium halecinum*, Skomer, Wales.

Studio shot of adult, Skomer, Wales.

Studio shot of adult and spawn on the hydroid *Halecium halecinum*, Skomer, Wales.

Rubramoena rubescens (Picton & Brown, 1978)

DESCRIPTION The full coloration of this nudibranch is only developed in adults. The cerata bases are flushed with red, and splashes of white pigment cover the dorsal surfaces of the cerata, becoming more continuous towards the tips. The rhinophores have a band of dark reddish pigment halfway up their length and are predominantly white above this. The dorsal surfaces of the oral tentacles have a continuous band of white pigment, and this distinguishing feature is present even in juveniles. Adults are normally about 12–15 mm in length.

ECOLOGY The food of this species is the hydroid *Halecium halecinum* and specimens may be found wherever this common hydroid occurs, usually on rock surfaces in semi-sheltered sites with some tidal stream movement. The spawn is a thin ribbon tangled amongst the hydroid branches.

DISTRIBUTION Found around Britain and Ireland and north to Norway.

SIMILAR SPECIES *Rubramoena amoena* (p. 240) is a closely allied species also feeding on *Halecium halecinum*. It has a brown band in the middle of the oral tentacles.

KEY CHARACTERISTICS Oral tentacles with white pigment on their dorsal surfaces. Red pigment at the bases of the cerata.

Adult on silty bedrock, Skomer, Wales.

Studio shot of adult, Connemara, Ireland.

Adult and spawn on the hydroid *Halecium halecinum*, Gulen, Norway.

Tenellia pallida (Alder & Hancock, 1845)

DESCRIPTION A tiny nudibranch with few cerata, arranged in groups of 2 or 3 along each side of the body. The pale brown body is marked with tiny black spots as are the cerata. The digestive gland is pale orange in colour. The oral tentacles are small and directed laterally. Grows up to 8 mm in length. The spawn consists of a short, curved, lozenge-shaped mass.

ECOLOGY Normally found in brackish localities with salinity as low as 3 parts per thousand. The animals feed on hydroids, especially *Cordylophora lacustris*, *Laomedea* species and *Protohydra leuckarti*.

DISTRIBUTION There are few records of *Tenellia pallida,* but it is probably widely distributed in estuarine conditions. Recent records are from the Bristol Channel and the Fleet in Dorset. In the middle of last century, it was common at Rotherhithe on the Thames, in London's dockland.

SIMILAR SPECIES The small size and few cerata make it possible to confuse this species with juveniles of other aeolids. This species has been synonymised with *Tenellia adspersa* (opposite, below) but recent DNA results and the description of *Tenellia gotlandica* (opposite) from Sweden (Korshunova *et al.*, 2023) bring this into question and more research is needed on this genus. *Bohuslania matsmichaeli* (p. 230) is another small nudibranch which is found in brackish water.

KEY CHARACTERISTICS Small lobes instead of normal oral tentacles. Cerata in rows of 2 or 3. Small black spots on body and cerata surfaces.

Tenellia pallida, Idde Fjord, Sweden. (Fredrik Pleijel)

Tenellia gotlandica, Sweden. (Klas Malmgren)

Tenellia adspersa, Northumberland, England. (Paula Lightfoot)

Trinchesia caerulea (Montagu, 1804)

DESCRIPTION This species is inconspicuous from a distance, but brightly coloured on close examination. The body is transparent and colourless, with some diffuse white pigment on the oral tentacles and rhinophores. The cerata have a core of green digestive gland, with bright blue pigment masking the upper region of the gland and yellow or orange surface pigment over the tip. Scattered yellow pigment is present below the blue region. The front of the foot is extended into recurved, rounded propodial tentacles. Typically, about 12 mm in length.

ECOLOGY Feeds on hydroids of the genus *Sertularella*, especially *Sertularella polyzonias.* The spawn is a thin, white, scalloped ribbon wound amongst the food.

DISTRIBUTION Found around Britain and Ireland, and from Scandinavia to the Mediterranean Sea.

SIMILAR SPECIES *Trinchesia cuanensis* (p. 248) and *Trinchesia morrowae* (p. 250) are very similar species only recently separated by DNA evidence and detailed morphological comparison (Korshunova *et al.*, 2019). Anatomically *Diaphoreolis viridis* (p. 238) is similar, but it has no orange or yellow tips to the cerata.

KEY CHARACTERISTICS Cerata with bright blue pigment in upper region, and a yellow or orange tip. Long propodial tentacles.

Studio shot of adult, Skomer, Wales.

Studio shot of adult, Connemara, Ireland.

Studio shot of spawn, Skomer, Wales.

Trinchesia cuanensis

Korshunova, Picton, Furfaro, Mariottini, Pontes, Prkić, Fletcher, Malmberg, Lundin & Martynov, 2019

DESCRIPTION Recently described as a new species previously confused with *Trinchesia caerulea*. The body is transparent and colourless, with some diffuse pale yellow pigment on the oral tentacles and rhinophores. The cerata are barrel-shaped and have a core of dark green digestive gland, with bright blue pigment masking the central region of the gland, a dark band followed by orange surface pigment over the cnidosac region and a transparent tip. The front of the foot is expanded slightly as blunt propodial tentacles. Typically, about 12 mm in length.

ECOLOGY Feeds on hydroids of the genus *Sertularella*, especially *Sertularella polyzonias*. The spawn is a coiled ribbon wound on the food.

DISTRIBUTION Found around Britain and Ireland, and from Scandinavia to the Mediterranean Sea.

SIMILAR SPECIES This species was formerly confused with *Trinchesia caerulea* (p. 246). It differs in the coloration of the cerata in having a dark band separating the blue from the orange region.

KEY CHARACTERISTICS Cerata with bright blue pigment in mid region, and an orange or red band above. Front of foot slightly expanded as blunt propodial tentacles.

Adult on the hydroid *Sertularella polyzonias*, Portrush, Northern Ireland.

Studio shot of adult, Orkney, Scotland.

Studio shot of adult and spawn on the hydroid *Sertularella polyzonias*, Lough Swilly, Ireland.

Trinchesia morrowae

Korshunova, Picton, Furfaro, Mariottini, Pontes, Prkić, Fletcher, Malmberg, Lundin & Martynov, 2019

DESCRIPTION This species is smaller than the other blue trinchesiids. The body is transparent with a yellow hue and with well-defined orange tips to the oral tentacles and rhinophores. There is a mid-dorsal stripe of opaque white pigment which runs from the front of the head as a broad band, between the rhinophores to divide around the heart region and continue as a thin line to the tail. The cerata have a core of dark green digestive gland, with bright blue pigment masking the central region of the gland and orange surface pigment over the outer third. A broad ring of orange is also present below the blue region. Typically, about 8 mm in length.

ECOLOGY Feeds on hydroids of the genus *Sertularella* and *Laomedea angulata*. The spawn is a small ribbon wound amongst the food.

DISTRIBUTION A southern species, found rarely in southern England and becoming common in the Mediterranean Sea.

SIMILAR SPECIES This species was formerly confused with *Trinchesia caerulea* (p. 246). It differs from the other species in this colour group in having a mid-dorsal opaque white line and orange tips to the head tentacles.

KEY CHARACTERISTICS Cerata with bright blue pigment in mid region, and an orange or yellow band above and below. Outer half of rhinophores and oral tentacles is orange. Line of opaque white pigment along centre line of head.

Adult *Trinchesia morrowae* on seagrass, Mediterranean coast of Spain. (Enric Madrenas)

Comparison studio shot of *Trinchesia caerulea* and *T. cuanensis*.

Adult *Trinchesia morrowae* with spawn on seagrass, Mediterranean coast of Spain. (Enric Madrenas)

Trinchesia foliata (Forbes & Goodsir, 1839)

DESCRIPTION This nudibranch has a complex pattern of red markings on the head and body. There are red rings on the oral tentacles and rhinophores, crescent-shaped red marks running longitudinally in front of and behind the rhinophore bases, and a red V-shaped mark behind the heart in the centre of the back. The body and cerata are flecked with spots of yellowish white pigment, which becomes almost continuous on the front of the head, and forms rings below the tips of the pointed cerata. Typically, 10 mm in length.

ECOLOGY This species seems to have a wider choice of hydroid food than most other *Trinchesia* species. It has certainly been shown to eat *Obelia* species and *Halecium* species and occurs beneath loose stones on the shore as well as in the sublittoral.

DISTRIBUTION Widespread in Britain and Ireland, recorded from the Faeroes, Norway, Portugal, Mediterranean coast of Spain and one record from the Azores.

SIMILAR SPECIES The markings on the head distinguish this species from other *Trinchesia* species apart from *Trinchesia genovae* (p. 253); the exact shape of the markings distinguish the latter.

KEY CHARACTERISTICS Five red markings in the head/heart region. Cerata and body with golden flecks of pigment.

Studio shot of adult, Connemara, Ireland.

Trinchesia genovae (O'Donoghue, 1926)

DESCRIPTION This nudibranch has a complex pattern of red markings on the head and body. The oral tentacles and rhinophores are yellow, with transparent tips and an orange ring just below the tip. The sides of the head and top of the head and heart region have patches of white pigment, and similar patches occur on the centre of the back and sides of the body. A tiny species, typically 6 mm in length when fully mature.

ECOLOGY This species has been found beneath rocks in exposed sites. It also occurs amongst masses of fouling ascidians and *Tubularia larynx* on floating structures and lines. The precise food requirements are unknown.

DISTRIBUTION Rare in Britain and Ireland, with records from Lough Hyne, Bantry Bay, Galway Bay and Connemara in western Ireland. May replace *Trinchesia foliata* in the Mediterranean Sea, where it is well known.

SIMILAR SPECIES The markings on the head distinguish this species from other *Trinchesia* species apart from *Trinchesia foliata* (p. 252).

KEY CHARACTERISTICS Red and white markings in the head/heart region. Yellow line down centre of head. Cerata stubby, with terminal rings of white and orange.

Studio shot of adult, Connemara, Ireland.

Zelentia pustulata (Alder & Hancock, 1854)

DESCRIPTION The cerata in this nudibranch are long and thin, giving a shaggy appearance. The digestive gland is normally coloured bright yellow, though this fades to a dull brown in starved animals. There are white pigment spots scattered over the surfaces of the cerata, and the rhinophores have white tips. The tail is long, thin, and transparent, but may often be damaged. Grows up to about 18 mm in length.

ECOLOGY Feeds on the hydroid *Halecium muricatum*, which has a yellow main stem. This hydroid is local in its distribution, occurring in scattered exposed localities in southwest Britain, west Ireland, and Scotland. It appears to be commoner in the north of Britain and Ireland, and the distribution of *Z. pustulata* reflects this. The spawn is a convoluted coil wound round the hydroid food.

DISTRIBUTION A northern species found as far south as Lundy Island in the Bristol Channel and Skomer Island in Wales, where it may be frequent. It has been recorded all along the Norwegian coast.

SIMILAR SPECIES The bright yellow digestive gland distinguishes this species from other aeolids. *Zelentia ninel* (opposite, below), has been found in northern Norway but is very small and lacks the white markings on the cerata, with just a few spots at the tip (Korshunova *et al.*, 2017c).

KEY CHARACTERISTICS Long, thin cerata with yellow digestive gland. Scattered white dots on surfaces of cerata.

Adult on bedrock with red seaweeds, Skomer, Wales.

Studio shot of adult, Mayo, Ireland.

Adult on the hydroid *Halecium muricatum*, Mayo, Ireland.

Zelentia ninel, Alta Fjord, Norway. (Erling Svensen)

Amphorina andra

Korshunova, Malmberg, Prkić, Petani, Fletcher, Lundin & Martynov, 2020

DESCRIPTION Previously confused with *Amphorina farrani*. This species has very swollen cerata and spots of orange or orange surrounded by black on the back. The rhinophores normally have a darker band within orange pigment in the upper third. The cerata often have smoky grey patches on the surface. There is an orange morph which is almost entirely translucent orange and a white morph which has only a small amount of opaque white pigment at the tips of the cerata and is otherwise translucent white. The tail has no white line down the centre. Grows to 20 mm in length.

ECOLOGY Usually found in the shallow subtidal, it feeds upon *Obelia geniculata* on kelp fronds and on other species of *Obelia*. The spawn is a ribbon, flared out on its upper margin.

DISTRIBUTION Found around Britain and Ireland and from Norway to the Mediterranean.

SIMILAR SPECIES Very similar to *Amphorina farrani* (p. 258). *Amphorina andra* tends to have more swollen cerata and brown rings are often present on the rhinophores. *A. viriola* (p. 264) is also very similar to this species (Korshunova *et al.*, 2020b).

KEY CHARACTERISTICS Swollen cerata with yellow or white bands of pigment at the tip. Pigment spots usually extensive on body. Smoky grey patches or occasionally black spots on cerata.

On kelp blade, Gulen, Norway.

Studio shot of adult, Connemara, Ireland.

Spawn coils on the hydroid *Obelia* sp., thin coil at centre is possibly *Dendronotus* sp., not *Amphorina andra*, Connemara, Ireland.

Amphorina farrani (Alder & Hancock, 1844)

DESCRIPTION The normal morph encountered is translucent white with scattered yellow patches on its dorsum. The tips of the cerata have yellow caps, and the outer half of the rhinophores and most of the oral tentacles are covered in yellow pigment. The translucent white skin can be replaced by a purple black. An all-white form with the orange pigment replaced by white is common. Mature specimens of *Amphorina farrani* grow to 20 mm in length. The spawn is a ribbon laid in a spiral of about 2 turns, flared out on its upper margin.

ECOLOGY Usually found in the shallow subtidal, it feeds on *Obelia dichotoma* and on *Aglaophenia pluma*.

DISTRIBUTION Found around Britain and Ireland and from Norway to the Mediterranean.

SIMILAR SPECIES The white morph with yellow-tipped cerata and tentacles is the form most likely to be confused with *Eubranchus tricolor* (p. 274); however *A. farrani* can be easily distinguished by the presence of yellow pigment on the rhinophores, oral tentacles and dorsum. Several other *Amphorina* species were previously identified as *A. farrani*.

KEY CHARACTERISTICS Moderately swollen cerata with broad yellow bands of pigment at the tip. Pigment spots usually on body but never on cerata. White centreline on tail and yellow tip to tail.

Two individuals on silty hydroids, Skomer, Wales.

Studio shot of adult, Skomer, Wales.

Ribbons of spawn on the hydroid *Obelia dichotoma*, Skomer, Wales.

Amphorina linensis (García-Gómez, Cervera & F. J. Garcia, 1990)

DESCRIPTION This species has several colour morphs. The most common morph encountered is translucent white with irregular orange patches on its back which are outlined in grey-brown. The tips of the cerata have opaque white pigment. The rhinophores and oral tentacles have a brown band in the upper half, with pale brown and white pigment above this. A white form with no orange or a few small orange-red spots is frequent. Most individuals have numerous small white spots on the surfaces of the cerata. The edge of the foot usually has minute white glands, but these can be rare in darker individuals. Mature specimens of *Amphorina linensis* grow to 20 mm in length.

ECOLOGY Frequently in heavily silted areas, it feeds upon *Obelia dichotoma* and other species of *Obelia*. The spawn is a ribbon, flared out on its upper margin.

DISTRIBUTION Found around Britain and Ireland and from Norway to the Mediterranean.

SIMILAR SPECIES Similar to *Amphorina andra* (p. 256), this species can be distinguished by the small white spots on the ceratal surfaces and the white line of glands at the edge of the foot.

KEY CHARACTERISTICS Amphora-shaped cerata with white bands or sparse white pigment at the tip. Small white spots on the cerata.

Adult of white form amongst mussels, Zeeland, Netherlands.

Studio shot of adult, Skomer, Wales.

Spawn coil, Zeeland, Netherlands.

Amphorina pallida (Alder & Hancock, 1842)

DESCRIPTION The body and ceratal surfaces are pigmented with white and brown-red patches, and there are yellow bands towards the tips of the cerata. The rhinophores and oral tentacles have a band of brown pigment and white pigment spots becoming dense at the tips. Alder & Hancock had a very pale individual as their type specimen, hence the somewhat inappropriate specific name; they later wanted to change the name to *picta* (painted). In Norway individuals with no brown pigment are common and look very different from typical *Amphorina pallida*. Adults may reach 23 mm in length.

ECOLOGY Feeds on calyptoblastic hydroids such as *Obelia dichotoma*, *Halecium halecinum* and *Halecium muricatum*.

DISTRIBUTION Recorded from around Britain and Ireland, the eastern seaboard of North America, Iceland and from Norway to the Mediterranean Sea.

SIMILAR SPECIES All *Amphorina* species (pp. 256–264) can be difficult to distinguish, but the brown speckled form of *A. pallida* is distinctive.

KEY CHARACTERISTICS Swollen cerata with yellow and white bands of pigment at the tip. Brown and yellow and white pigment spots on body and cerata.

Two individuals, one pale and the other highly pigmented, on kelp blade, Gulen, Norway.

Studio shot of adult, Gulen, Norway.

Two individuals and spawn, Gulen, Norway.

Amphorina viriola

Korshunova, Malmberg, Prkić, Petani, Fletcher, Lundin & Martynov, 2020

DESCRIPTION This species is not distinguishable from *Amphorina andra* by DNA barcodes. It is similar to that species in appearance but always has a band of pink glandular pigment at the tips of the cerata. There is usually light brown, smoky grey or olive green pigment in patches over the back. The cerata are less inflated than in *A. andra* and often have a smoky grey hue with opaque white flecks in the outer third. Specimens with some orange pigment at the centre of the spots on the back and at the tips of the cerata are known. Grows to 12 mm in length.

ECOLOGY Usually found in very shallow water.

DISTRIBUTION Found in brackish water at the entrance to the Baltic Sea in Denmark and Sweden.

SIMILAR SPECIES The morph with olive green pigment patches is most easily distinguished from other *Amphorina* species (pp. 256–262). The presence of sparse opaque white flecks on the outer parts of the cerata seems to be a feature of this species.

KEY CHARACTERISTICS Swollen cerata with a band of pink pigment at the tip. Pigment patches with darker or orange centres usually on body. Flecks of opaque white on the cerata.

Adult on red weed, Resö, Sweden. (Michael Lundin)

Studio shot of adult, Lysekil, Denmark. (Poul Eric Rasmussen)

Studio shot of adult, Lysekil, Denmark. (Poul Eric Rasmussen)

Capellinia fustifera (Lovén, 1846)

Previously *Eubranchus doriae* (Trinchese, 1874)

DESCRIPTION This is a small nudibranch, with adults only growing to about 12 mm. The body is translucent white, with scattered brown or green pigment on the back and cerata. The cerata have 2 or 3 rows of tubercles. The tip of each ceras is covered by a pale patch and encircled by a brown-coloured ring. The rhinophoral and oral tentacles are smooth; the tips of these tentacles are white with a subterminal brown band.

ECOLOGY This species feeds on the plumulariid hydroid *Kirchenpaueria similis*, which is like a smaller, finer version of *Kirchenpaueria pinnata*. The spawn is similar to *Eubranchus vittatus*.

DISTRIBUTION Few records exist for this species; however it has been found around the southern and western coasts of Britain and Ireland, Lundy Island and Pagham Harbour, Sussex, north to Mulroy Bay, County Donegal and St Kilda, off the west coast of Scotland. It occurs in southern Norway and in the Mediterranean Sea.

SIMILAR SPECIES *Capellinia fustifera* is sometimes confused with *Eubranchus vittatus* (p. 276) but may be readily distinguished by the presence of tubercles on the cerata; *Eubranchus exiguus* (p. 268) and *Eubranchus scintillans* (p. 272) are both similar to this species, but smaller and with only one swollen region of the cerata.

KEY CHARACTERISTICS Cerata with irregular swellings over outgrowths of digestive gland. Body with green patches.

On kelp stipe with epiphytic hydroids and bryozoans, Gulen, Norway.

Studio shot of adult, Skomer, Wales.

Numerous spawn coils amongst bryozoan turf, Skomer, Wales.

Eubranchus exiguus (Alder & Hancock, 1848)

DESCRIPTION The body is translucent white with patches of brown or green pigment. The cerata are few in number and slightly swollen in the middle. They have 2 bands of pigment patches. The rhinophoral and oral tentacles have a subterminal ring of white pigment and lower down, towards their base, 1 or sometimes 2 bands of brown pigment. Adults may grow to 10 mm in length. The spawn consists of lozenge-shaped lumps.

ECOLOGY Often found in large numbers forming mixed populations with *Tergipes tergipes* feeding on *Obelia geniculata* on kelp fronds.

DISTRIBUTION Found around Britain and Ireland, and from the Arctic, Scandinavia, and the Mediterranean.

SIMILAR SPECIES Possible confusion with *Eubranchus scintillans* (p. 272) and *Capellinia fustifera* (p. 266) but can be distinguished by its banded, not spotted, cerata. *Tergipes tergipes* (p. 228) has cerata which are single, not in rows, and *Eubranchus rupium* (p. 270) has thinner cerata and orange-brown spots.

KEY CHARACTERISTICS Cerata few in number, fusiform in shape. Green pigment patches on body and on cerata.

On kelp with hydroids, Strangford Lough, Ireland.

Studio shot of adult, Isle of Man.

Spawn on hydroids on kelp blade, Isle of Man.

Eubranchus rupium (Møller, 1842)

DESCRIPTION The body is translucent white with scattered brown pigment spots. The cerata are in about 6 or 7 rows with 1–3 in each row. The green/brown digestive gland within the body is visible as a zigzag line connecting the cerata bases in the back of the body. The cerata have white tips composed of many small spots and there are elongate brown-red markings on the sides of the cerata which are often paired. These markings may form a band where there is a constriction in the ceras, about a quarter of the way down from the tip. The rhinophoral and oral tentacles have scattered opaque white pigment at the tips, an indistinct band of brown pigment and some brown and white spots in the inner half. Adults may grow to 12 mm in length.

ECOLOGY Reported to feed on shallow water hydroids such as *Obelia* and *Bougainvillea* species. The spawn is a short, curved ribbon.

DISTRIBUTION A northern species, recorded from Iceland, Scandinavia, Denmark and the North Sea. Tolerant of lowered salinity.

SIMILAR SPECIES *Eubranchus rupium* is most likely to be confused with *Eubranchus scintillans* (p. 272) or *Eubranchus exiguus* (p. 268), but it has thin, cylindrical cerata and different pigmentation.

KEY CHARACTERISTICS Cerata few in number, cylindrical or slightly swollen in the outer half. Brown pigment patches on body and on cerata.

On kelp blade, Egersund, Norway. (Erling Svensen)

Studio shot of adult, Gulen, Norway. (Christian Skauge)

On kelp with *Obelia geniculata*, Egersund, Norway. (Erling Svensen)

Eubranchus scintillans Grishina, Schepetov & Ekimova, 2022

Recently split from *Eubranchus exiguus.*

DESCRIPTION The body is translucent white with spots of olive brown pigment on the back which coalesce into patches on the sides. The cerata are few in number with a swelling at the middle created by lateral extensions of the digestive gland. The surfaces of the cerata have round spots of brown pigment distributed evenly over them. The rhinophoral and oral tentacles have a ring of white pigment near the tip. Adults may grow to 10 mm in length.

ECOLOGY Feeds on shallow water hydroids such as *Obelia dichotoma* and species of *Laomedea*. The spawn consists of lozenge-shaped lumps.

DISTRIBUTION Found around Britain and Ireland, and from the Arctic and Scandinavia.

SIMILAR SPECIES Recently distinguished from *Eubranchus exiguus* (p. 268) by DNA sequencing and subsequent analysis of external and internal features. The shape of the cerata and round, olive green spots are distinctive. *Eubranchus rupium* (p. 270) has probably been confused with this species in the past; it has slim cerata.

KEY CHARACTERISTICS Cerata few in number, urn shaped. Olive green pigment spots on body and on cerata.

Adult amongst hydroids, Gulen, Norway.

Adult amongst hydroids, Gulen, Norway.

Spawn packets of *Eubranchus scintillans*, Mulroy Bay, Donegal, Ireland.

Eubranchus tricolor

Forbes, 1838

DESCRIPTION The body is translucent white in colour and may reach up to 45 mm in length. The cerata are extremely numerous, flattened and swollen. The brown digestive gland is clearly visible through the translucent epidermis of the cerata and becomes purple just below the cnidosac. The cerata have a sub-terminal ring of yellow pigment, with a white ring below this. The rhinophores and oral tentacles are devoid of pigment.

ECOLOGY *Eubranchus tricolor* is reported to feed on both gymnoblastic and calyptoblastic hydroids. In Britain it is often found in large numbers on *Nemertesia ramosa* colonies during the summer months, and it has been observed on *Diphasia margareta* and other sertulariid hydroids. An aberrant form has been frequently found on *Tubularia indivisa* in the spring.

DISTRIBUTION This species occurs around Britain and Ireland, America, Greenland, the Faeroes and Scandinavia. The most southerly record is from the Atlantic coast of France; and Mediterranean records have been shown to be *Amphorina andra*.

SIMILAR SPECIES Possible confusion with *Amphorina* species (pp. 256–264).

KEY CHARACTERISTICS Swollen cerata with yellow or white bands of pigment at the tips. No pigment spots on body or cerata.

Adult on the hydroid *Halecium halecinum*, entrance to Lough Foyle, Northern Ireland.

Studio shot of adult, Lunga, western Scotland.

Spawn coil on the hydroid *Tubularia indivisa*, Gulen, Norway.

Eubranchus vittatus (Alder & Hancock, 1842)

DESCRIPTION This nudibranch is greyish white in colour with scattered patches of green or brown pigment. Each ceras has a white band towards its tip and 2 or 3 green or brown bands below this. The digestive gland is white and is visible through the ceratal epidermis. The rhinophores are smooth with white tips and a lower green or brown band. The larger individuals may grow to a length of approximately 20 mm.

ECOLOGY *Eubranchus vittatus* feeds on the calyptoblastic hydroid *Kirchenpaueria pinnata*. The spawn consists of a flared, cup-like circle of white ribbon with a basal pad attaching it to the hydroid stem.

DISTRIBUTION A frequent species in the northwest of Britain and Ireland but much scarcer further south. It has been reported from southern Norway, Sweden and the Netherlands; the most southern record appears to be Galicia in northwest Spain.

SIMILAR SPECIES This species is similar in appearance to *Capellinia fustifera* (p. 266) but has smooth, unswollen cerata with bands of dark pigment.

KEY CHARACTERISTICS Cerata not swollen, in vertical rows. Cerata with dark bands, green pigment and white spots on body.

On the hydroid *Kirchenpaueria pinnata*, Isle of Man.

Studio shot, Isle of Man.

Numerous spawn coils on the hydroid *Kirchenpaueria pinnata*, Connemara, Ireland.

Cumanotus beaumonti (Eliot, 1906)

DESCRIPTION This is a beautiful and rare aeolid, with long flowing cerata. The body is translucent with speckles of gold pigment on the dorsum and concentrated into patches on the head. The cerata taper smoothly from broad bases to fine tips. They are translucent, with the brown digestive gland showing clearly in the basal region but becoming very thin distally. There are elongate cnidosacs in the tips of the cerata. Flecks of gold pigment decorate the upper surfaces of the cerata. The cerata are muscular and the animal is capable of swimming by vigorous flexing of the body.

ECOLOGY This species feeds on the hydroid *Corymorpha nutans*, a large athecate hydroid which grows as single individuals on sand or gravel seabeds. It may also be found feeding on *Tubularia indivisa* or *Ectopleura larynx*.

DISTRIBUTION Records of this species are scarce. Recently it has been found in Northern Ireland and western Scotland; the original locality was Plymouth, and it was found at the same time in Norway. It is quite frequent in Norwegian fjords.

SIMILAR SPECIES The combination of the very broad foot and long cerata make this species obviously different from *Gulenia* and *Facelina* species. *Xenocratena suecica* (p. 284) is another species adapted for life on sediment seabeds, with a broad foot.

KEY CHARACTERISTICS Numerous tapering long cerata. Transparent body with gold speckles of pigment.

Adult feeding on the hydroid *Corymorpha nutans*, Egersund, Norway. (Erling Svensen)

Studio shot of adult, Rathlin Island, Northern Ireland. (Fred Pleijel)

Spawn coil anchored in muddy sand, Rathlin Island, Northern Ireland.

Fiona pinnata (Eschscholtz, 1831)

DESCRIPTION This is another ocean wanderer like *Scyllaea pelagica* which rarely turns up stranded on our shores. The body is pale fawn in colour with white speckling. The numerous cerata contain coloured digestive gland which may be brown if the animal has been feeding on goose barnacles or blue if the food has been the siphonophore *Velella velella*.

ECOLOGY *Fiona pinnata* lives at the surface of the sea, feeding on goose barnacles attached to floating debris or on free-living siphonophores such as the By-the-wind Sailor *Velella velella*.

DISTRIBUTION The distribution of this species is circumtropical, found in both the Atlantic and the Indo-Pacific basins. It really lives in the open ocean, like *Scyllaea pelagica* (p. 154), but has been found cast up on shores in western Europe.

SIMILAR SPECIES This is the only aeolid nudibranch with gill leaves on the cerata.

KEY CHARACTERISTICS Numerous cerata with thin undulating margins on their posterior edges. Digestive gland blue or brown, body colourless.

Adult on plastic debris, Cala Rajada, Mallorca, Spain. (David Martinez)

Adult on plastic debris, Cala Rajada, Mallorca, Spain. (David Martinez)

Two adults with spawn coils on plastic debris, Cala Rajada, Mallorca, Spain. (David Martinez)

Pseudovermis boadeni Salvini-Plawen & Sterrer, 1968

DESCRIPTION This tiny worm-like nudibranch will only be found by using special techniques for collection of meiofauna – animals which live between sand grains. The cerata are reduced to swellings along the sides of the body and are mostly composed of cnidosacs. The body is transparent. There are rudimentary rhinophores and conspicuous eyes. The body length reaches 3.5 mm.

ECOLOGY Feeds on the interstitial hydroid *Halammohydra vermiformis.*

DISTRIBUTION Apparently known only from the original locality on Anglesey, and from the Bristol Channel. Unlikely to be encountered except by deliberate searching, so may be more widespread.

SIMILAR SPECIES DNA evidence suggests that this is a paedomorphic species, and the closest family to Pseudovermidae is Cumanotidae. Eleven other species of *Pseudovermis* are known worldwide.

KEY CHARACTERISTICS Worm-like animal with acorn-shaped head. Cerata reduced to swellings on sides of body.

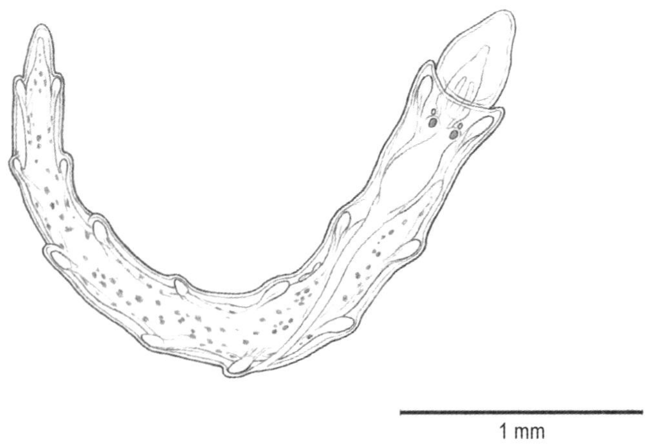

Pseudovermis boadeni (based on Thompson & Brown 1984, Thompson 1988).

Interstitial sea slugs

A habitat which has been colonised by some sea slugs is the space between sand grains on beaches and the seabed. This habitat is called mesopsammic or interstitial from the interstices, spaces, between sand grains. Different sizes of sand grains support different species of animals and these include polychaete worms, molluscs, nematodes, crustacea and cnidaria as well as lesser known groups which specialise on this sort of habitat such as kinorhynchs. One nudibranch family with this habit is the Pseudovermidae – translated this means false worms. The pseudovermids are aeolid nudibranchs with cerata and cnidosacs and they feed on cnidarians which are present between the sand grains, such as *Halammohydra* species.

There is another group of sea slugs, the acochlids, which are all interstitial animals. A number of species have been found in our area, but not all have names yet. The range of morphology is illustrated here by *Asperspina brambelli*, *Hedylopsis spiculifera*, and *Microhedyle glandulifera*.

Embletonia pulchra (p. 158) is also considered to be an interstitial animal, but is probably intermediate in habitat as it has often been found clinging underneath stones lying on sand.

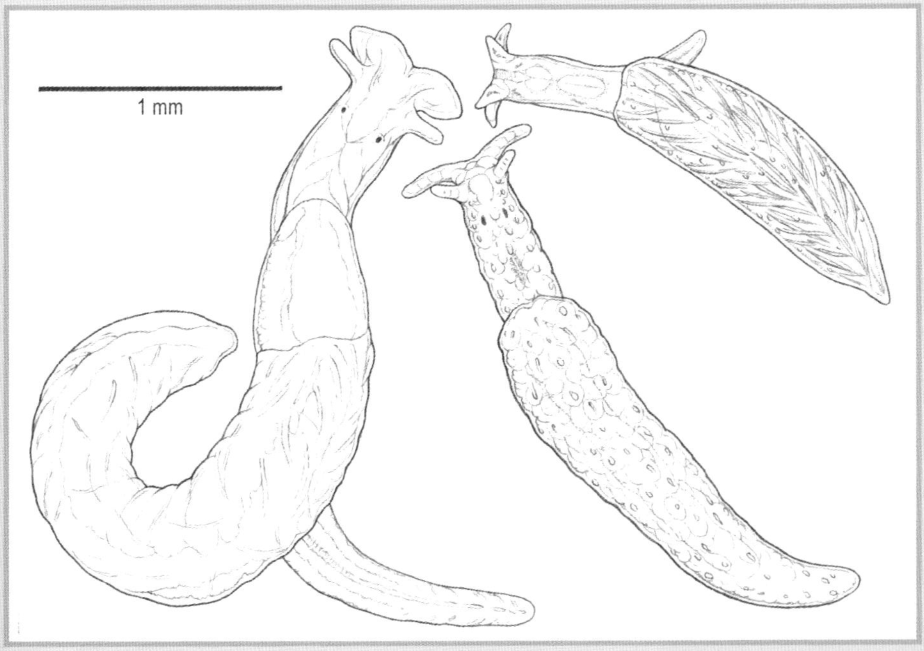

Left to right: *Asperspina brambelli*, *Microhedyle glandulifera* and *Hedylopsis spiculifera* (*A. brambelli* based on Thompson 1988).

Xenocratena suecica

Odhner, 1940

DESCRIPTION The body is translucent with scattered spots of opaque white pigment on the front of the head and the back. The rhinophores are smooth with a few white flecks near the tips. The oral tentacles are longer than the width of the body. The digestive gland is visible through the ceratal epidermis and is rose red in colour. The largest cerata have a few surface speckles of opaque white. Can grow to 12 mm in length.

ECOLOGY This uncommon species is known from sediment seabeds below 20 m depth. The food is unknown, but the sea pen *Virgularia mirabilis* and the hydroid *Corymorpha nutans* are two cnidarians characteristic of the habitat. The animals are able to burrow rapidly into the seabed when disturbed by a diver's torch.

DISTRIBUTION Apparently rare and only known from a few sheltered sites in Norway and Sweden.

SIMILAR SPECIES The broad foot and overall appearance are similar to *Cumanotus beaumonti* (p. 278).

KEY CHARACTERISTICS Translucent animal with sparse white speckles on the body and cerata. Rhinophores smooth. Oral tentacles longer than width of the body.

Small individual on muddy seabed, Hafrsfjord, Norway. (Erling Svensen)

Adult on muddy seabed, Norway. (Rudolph Svensen)

Adult burrowing into the seabed, northeast of Stavanger, Norway. (Rudolph Svensen)

Calma glaucoides (Alder & Hancock, 1854)

DESCRIPTION The cerata are arranged in up to 12 neat clusters with 4 cerata per cluster. The long cerata have bluish white pigment over the dorsal surfaces, and the animals have yellowish tips to the cerata, oral tentacles and rhinophores. The foot is broad, with well-developed propodial tentacles. In mature specimens the rosette-like structures of the ovotestis show clearly through the transparent back. Grows to about 23 mm in length.

ECOLOGY Feeds on the eggs of cephalopods and fish, especially those of clingfish. These eggs are usually laid beneath rocks or shells.

DISTRIBUTION There are a few scattered records of this species from the coasts of Britain and Ireland; elsewhere it has been recorded from Norway, the Atlantic coasts of France, Spain, and Portugal as well as the Mediterranean Sea.

SIMILAR SPECIES Old records of this species include *Calma gobioophaga* (p. 288) which is a smaller animal with short, bulbous cerata.

KEY CHARACTERISTICS Numerous cerata in groups of 4 along sides of body. Transparent body with ovotestis lobules showing through back. Long bluish cerata with yellow tips.

In rockpool, Cornwall, England. (Michiel Vos)

Studio shot of juvenile, Connemara, Ireland.

In rockpool, Cornwall, England. (Michiel Vos)

Calma gobioophaga

Calado & Urgorri, 2002

DESCRIPTION This small aeolid grows to a maximum length of 16 mm but is generally between 8 and 12 mm. The body, rhinophores and cerata are all translucent greyish yellow. The stomach and ovotestis are visible through the transparent body. The white ovotestis is divided into paired lateral groups arranged at the base of each ceratal bunch. The colour of the stomach and rhinophore depends on the type of food eaten. The cerata are arranged in clusters of 2–4 but generally 3; the cerata are fusiform in shape with mucronate tips. There is a dense band of white spots just below the tip of the cerata. The rhinophores and oral tentacles are smooth with some opaque white pigment on the surfaces near the tip.

ECOLOGY Feeds on the eggs of the black goby *Gobius niger*. As many as 50 or 60 *Calma* have been found on a single batch of eggs. A fine spiral ribbon of eggs is laid amongst the fish eggs.

DISTRIBUTION Originally described from Portugal, this species has recently been recorded from the south coast of England.

SIMILAR SPECIES Recently separated from *Calma glaucoides* (p. 286), this is a much slimmer animal with short cerata.

KEY CHARACTERISTICS Numerous cerata in groups of 4 along sides of body. Transparent body with ovotestis lobules showing through back. Short colourless cerata.

Adult and spawn on goby eggs, Dorset, England. (Steve Trewhella)

In rockpool, Cornwall, England. (Michiel Vos)

Adult with goby eggs, in rockpool, Cornwall, England. (Michiel Vos)

Babakina anadoni (Ortea, 1979)

DESCRIPTION The body, rhinophores and oral tentacles of this distinctive aeolid are deep translucent pink. The tips of the rhinophores and oral tentacles are white. The lamellate rhinophores are relatively large and broad and fused at the base. The brightly coloured cerata have a band of bright yellow sandwiched between a band of purplish blue towards the base and a pinkish red band at the tip.

ECOLOGY On exposed coasts from the intertidal to the shallow subtidal, thought to feed on the hydroid *Candelabrum cocksii*.

DISTRIBUTION Atlantic coasts of France, Spain and Portugal, Straits of Gibraltar. Until 2022 the furthest north that this species had been seen was northern Spain. Two observations were recorded for England in 2022, one from the Isles of Scilly and one from the shore in Cornwall, and the first record for the Atlantic coast of France was recorded from Saint-Yves, Brittany. This species also occurs on the Atlantic coast of the USA.

SIMILAR SPECIES This is a very distinctive species.

KEY CHARACTERISTICS Rhinophores fused at the base. Distinctive coloration.

Adult on bryozoan encrusted bedrock with the tentacles of the hydroid *Candelabrum cocksii* visible, Isles of Scilly, England. (Allen Murray)

Studio shot of the hydroid *Candelabrum cocksii*, Looe, Cornwall, England.

Animal with spawn coil beneath rock, Florida, USA. (Ariane Dimitris)

Caloria elegans (Alder & Hancock, 1845)

DESCRIPTION This rare nudibranch has a translucent white body with thin lines of superficial white pigment on the frontal surfaces of the rhinophores and the oral tentacles. The sides and rear surfaces of the rhinophores are ornamented with rounded tubercles. The line on the oral tentacles continues across the front of the head, and there is a line along the middle of the tail. The digestive gland is orange or pink in colour with a black area at the base of each ceras and a black glandular area just below the cnidosac. The cerata have white terminal rings, and the largest ones have long curled tips. The spawn is a thin thread deposited in a spiral.

ECOLOGY The diet of this species is unknown, but it has been found amongst the hydroids *Nemertesia ramosa*, *Plumularia setacea* and *Halecium halecinum*.

DISTRIBUTION Originally described from Torbay, this species has also been found at scattered sites around Britain and Ireland. It is currently synonymised with *Caloria maculata* which is quite a common species in the Mediterranean Sea.

SIMILAR SPECIES *Caloria quatrefagesi* has been recently separated from *Caloria elegans* by DNA studies and the fact that it has lamellate rhinophores (Furfaro *et al.*, 2016a). This brings into question the possibility that *C. maculata* is also a distinct species. These two species are found from Portugal southwards and not included here.

KEY CHARACTERISTICS Cerata with subterminal black glands. White line on oral tentacles continuous across front of head.

Adult with the hydroid *Nemertesia antennina*, The Maidens, Northern Ireland.

The unusual papillate rhinophores are clearly visible in this photo, The Maidens, Northern Ireland.

Adult and spawn on hydroid, Lough Swilly, Ireland.

Dicata odhneri

Schmekel, 1967

DESCRIPTION This tiny species is entirely covered with speckles of white pigment, becoming translucent in the heart region and in patches at the bases of the cerata. The rhinophores and oral tentacles are contrasting primrose yellow in their distal portions, and translucent in their basal halves. The body may reach 13 mm in length but is very thin and difficult to see in the field. The spawn is a fine spiral of eggs.

ECOLOGY The diet is unknown. In Lough Hyne the animals are found on silty rock in 6–10 m of water amongst algae, sponges and white didemnid sea squirts.

DISTRIBUTION This rare species is known only from Lough Hyne in County Cork, Portugal, and scattered records in the Mediterranean Sea. In Lough Hyne it has been found on several occasions since its discovery in 1980 and appears to maintain a resident population.

SIMILAR SPECIES Unlikely to be confused with other aeolids.

KEY CHARACTERISTICS Tiny aeolid with white superficial pigment. Rhinophores and oral tentacles with yellow pigment.

Adult amongst silty hydroids, Lough Hyne, Ireland.

Studio shot, Lough Hyne, Ireland.

Studio shot, side view, Lough Hyne, Ireland.

Facelina annulicornis (Chamisso & Eysenhardt, 1821)

DESCRIPTION The body is translucent with scattered spots of white pigment. Around the mouth the skin has a rose-coloured hue. The rhinophores are lamellate, both the rhinophoral and oral tentacles are tipped with white pigment. The digestive gland is visible through the ceratal epidermis, it may be brown, orange, or green in colour. The adults can grow to 40 mm in length.

ECOLOGY This uncommon species is known to feed on a variety of hydroids including *Halecium halecinum*, and to attack and devour other nudibranchs, especially species of Flabellinidae and Coryphellidae.

DISTRIBUTION Recorded from scattered sites in Britain and Ireland, the Atlantic coast of France, Portugal, and the Mediterranean Sea.

SIMILAR SPECIES This is a distinctive species due to its rhinophore colour and spots on the body and cerata. *Pruvotfolia pselliotes* (p. 308) is similar but has much smaller spots on the body and cerata.

KEY CHARACTERISTICS Brown animal with regular white speckles all over body and cerata. Rhinophores with sloping lamellae.

Adult on hydroid, Skomer, Wales.

Studio shot, Pembrokeshire, Wales.

Adult and spawn on the hydroid *Eudendrium* sp., Skomer, Wales.

Facelina auriculata (O F Müller, 1776)

DESCRIPTION When fully grown this nudibranch may reach 38 mm in length. The ground colour is translucent white and there is a rose-coloured hue around the mouth. The animal's red oesophagus is visible, just behind the rhinophores. There is an iridescent blue sheen on the head and ceratal surfaces that is characteristic of the species, but better developed in animals from deeper water. The oral tentacles are very long and the rhinophores are annulate. There are streaks of white pigment on both sets of tentacles. The cerata are also streaked with white, as is the tail of the animal.

ECOLOGY Known to feed on several hydroid species but has mainly been found on *Obelia geniculata* on kelp fronds and on *Tubularia indivisa*. Will sometimes eat smaller nudibranchs such as *Microchlamylla gracilis*. Found under boulders on shore as well as in the sublittoral.

DISTRIBUTION Recorded from around Britain and Ireland and from Norway to the Mediterranean.

SIMILAR SPECIES Possible confusion with *Facelina bostoniensis* (p. 300) but in *Facelina auriculata* the foot and body are more elongate and there is usually more blue iridescence.

KEY CHARACTERISTICS Propodial tentacles, long oral tentacles and annulate rhinophores present. Foot narrow, cerata short, in distinct bunches, long narrow tail. Cerata with red digestive gland and iridescent blue surface colour.

Feeding on *Microchlamylla gracilis*, Saltstraumen, Norway.

Studio shot of adult, Skomer, Wales.

Adult and spawn on red seaweed, Skomer, Wales.

Facelina bostoniensis (Couthouy, 1838)

DESCRIPTION The epidermis is translucent white. As in *Facelina auriculata*, there is a rose-coloured hue around the mouth. The red oesophagus, situated just behind the rhinophores, is clearly visible. There are a few patches of white pigment on the head, between the rhinophores and down the tail of the animal. Sometimes blue iridescence is present in small areas around the head. The rhinophores are annulate, the oral tentacles are very long, both sets of tentacles are tipped with white pigment. Brown digestive gland is visible through the cerata epidermis. Large individuals may grow to approximately 55 mm.

ECOLOGY In the sublittoral region this animal may be found on *Tubularia indivisa* and *Ectopleura larynx*; however it is often found on the low shore on *Clava multicornis* and probably eats several athecate hydroid species.

DISTRIBUTION Known from the northeast coast of America and from Norway to the Mediterranean.

SIMILAR SPECIES Similar in appearance to *F. auriculata* (p. 298), but *Facelina bostoniensis* has a much broader body and usually there is only a small amount of blue iridescence. *Facelina dubia* (p. 302) is similar but has smooth rhinophores with characteristic pigment on their frontal surfaces.

KEY CHARACTERISTICS Propodial tentacles, long oral tentacles and annulate rhinophores present. Foot broad and cerata long, overlapping, extending beyond tail. Cerata with streaks of white pigment but usually without blue iridescence.

Adult on the brown seaweed *Halidrys siliquosa* with the hydroid *Obelia* sp., Gulen, Norway.

The annulate rhinophores can be clearly seen in this photo, Gulen, Norway.

Spawn coil on the hydroid *Tubularia indivisa*, Gulen, Norway.

Facelina dubia

Pruvot-Fol, 1949

DESCRIPTION The body is translucent white with a pinkish hue over the head and tentacles. The red oesophagus is visible through the epidermis. Often there is a small patch of white pigment between the rhinophores. White speckling is present on the head, rhinophores, oral tentacles and cerata. The tips of the cerata are covered with yellow or white pigment. The oral tentacles are very long and mobile and the rhinophores are smooth. Adult specimens usually range from 17 to 38 mm in length.

ECOLOGY Thought to feed on *Ectopleura larynx* and possibly other hydroids. It is often found in places with high levels of silt and seems to be tolerant of lowered salinity.

DISTRIBUTION This seems to be a genuinely rare species. It has been regularly recorded in Lough Hyne, southwest Ireland; elsewhere it has been reported from Arcachon in the Bay of Biscay and the Mediterranean Sea. This species has also been photographed on several occasions in southern Norway and seen in Denmark, suggesting a wide temperature tolerance.

SIMILAR SPECIES *Facelina bostoniensis* (p. 300) is similar, but the annulate rhinophores of *F. bostoniensis* distinguish it from *Facelina dubia*.

KEY CHARACTERISTICS Propodial tentacles, long oral tentacles and smooth rhinophores present. Cerata with patches of dark surface pigment.

Adult on sediment covered rock, Egersund, Norway. (Erling Svensen)

Studio shot of adult, Lough Hyne, Ireland.

Adult, and spawn of a *Doto* species, on hydroid, Lough Hyne, Ireland.

Favorinus blianus

Lemche & Thompson, 1974

DESCRIPTION This nudibranch is translucent white with broken lines of white surface pigment on the cerata and along the midline of the back. There are 3 large annulations on each rhinophore. The distal portions of the rhinophores and the long oral tentacles are pigmented with white.

ECOLOGY This species feeds on the eggs of other nudibranchs and is likely to be found in small numbers wherever other nudibranchs are abundant. It lays a convoluted white string of eggs, normally coiled around hydroid stems.

DISTRIBUTION Found more commonly on the north and west coasts of Britain and Ireland, this species is recorded from Norway and as far south as Galicia in northwest Spain.

SIMILAR SPECIES *Favorinus vitreus* (not included here) is a species from the Canary Islands which has 2 annulations on the rhinophores, which are brown with white tips like *Favorinus branchialis* (p. 306).

KEY CHARACTERISTICS Rhinophores with 3 conspicuous annulations. White surface pigment in dotted or broken lines.

Adult eating *Doto hydrallmaniae* spawn on *Hydrallmania falcata*, Strangford Lough, Northern Ireland.

Studio shot, Gulen, Norway.

On coralline encrusted rock, Gulen, Norway.

Favorinus branchialis (Rathke, 1806)

DESCRIPTION This uncommon nudibranch has a translucent white body with extensive white surface pigment. The pigment forms a triangle on the head, with diamond-shaped patches down the centre of the back. The upper surfaces of the cerata are usually covered with white pigment but may be translucent, showing the white, brown, or orange digestive gland. The rhinophores are distinctive, being brown in the basal portion, with a swelling near the tip, and a white tip.

ECOLOGY *Favorinus* species feed on the spawn of other nudibranchs and are likely to be encountered wherever nudibranchs are abundant. The animals can be well camouflaged on large dorid egg masses. Juveniles feed on hydroids such as *Obelia*. The spawn of this species is a thin thread wound like a hair spring.

DISTRIBUTION Widely distributed in Britain and Ireland but rather local and scattered. This species is also known from the Mediterranean Sea to Norway.

SIMILAR SPECIES *Favorinus vitreus* (not included here) is a species from the Canary Islands which also has brown rhinophores with white tips; however in *F. vitreus* the cerata have 2 annulations.

KEY CHARACTERISTICS Rhinophores with brown shafts, a subterminal swelling and white tips. White pigment around the heart and along the midline of the back.

Adult feeding on nudibranch spawn, Skomer, Wales.

Studio shot, Skomer, Wales.

Two individuals, well hidden in the folds of the spawn coil of *Doris pseudoargus*, Strangford Lough, Northern Ireland.

Pruvotfolia pselliotes (Labbé, 1923)

DESCRIPTION This nudibranch has a translucent grey to brown body with small opaque white spots sprinkled all over the head and back. The cerata are translucent grey showing the thin grey digestive gland, or in more pigmented individuals there may be 2 white bands and white tips. The base of the digestive gland may be brown. The largest cerata in the middle of the back are very long and normally held in a partially coiled position. These cerata are straightened and waved vigorously if the animal is disturbed. The rhinophores have small sloping lamellae. The spawn of this species is a thin spiral ribbon.

ECOLOGY *Pruvotfolia pselliotes* can be found from the lower shore to 25 m depth on exposed to moderately exposed coasts. They are nocturnal, hiding in crevices or beneath rocks in the daytime and fleeing from light if disturbed. They feed on hydroids such as *Obelia*, *Kirchenpaueria*, *Sertularia* and *Tubularia* species as well as eating other nudibranchs such as *Doto* species.

DISTRIBUTION This species was described from southern Brittany. It was first seen in Britain in 2014 and immediately became quite common in the Torbay area. It has now been seen at sites on the south and north coasts of Cornwall. It has been reported from Croatia, the Canary Islands and Morocco.

SIMILAR SPECIES The coiled cerata are similar to the larger cerata of *Caloria elegans* (p. 292) and the overall appearance is somewhat similar to *Facelina annulicornis* (p. 296).

KEY CHARACTERISTICS Largest cerata held in a coiled position in the middle of the back, highly muscular. Fine white spots all over the dorsal surfaces.

Individual on underside of a boulder in a rockpool, Jersey, Channel Islands. (Nicolas Jouault)

Adult resting on a hydroid; the coiled cerata in the middle of the back are very obvious, Torbay, England. (Terry Griffiths)

Large individual on the hydroid *Kirchenpaueria pinnata* with *Doto dunnei* and its spawn. *Pruvotfolia pselliotes* may be eating the *Doto*. Torbay, England. (Terry Griffiths)

Aeolidia filomenae

Kienberger, Carmona, Pola, Padula, Gosliner & Cervera, 2016

DESCRIPTION This is a relatively large aeolid; most individuals are between 50 and 60 mm in length. It is usually greyish brown in colour due to specking of grey or brown pigment on the body and cerata, but pigmentation can be variable. There is a distinctive V-shaped white mark on the front of the head with its base between the rhinophores and arms running out to the oral tentacles. The rhinophores are greyish brown in colour with paler, usually cream-white tips. The cerata curve inwards in a C shape and are somewhat flattened. The spawn is similar to that of *Aeolidia papillosa*, consisting of a thread coiled back and forth and laid in a spiral.

ECOLOGY *Aeolidia filomenae* feeds on sea anemones, taking a wide variety of species, and is often found in the intertidal zone. The normal prey is *Actinia equina*, though *Anemonia viridis* is also taken.

DISTRIBUTION This species has been reported from Scotland south to Atlantic Spain and France but appears to be replaced by *A. papillosa* in colder waters.

SIMILAR SPECIES This species was previously confused with *A. papillosa* (p. 312) but is now known to be a distinct species. *A. papillosa* has uniform mottled coloration on the head and no pale V-shaped mark, and the cerata are almost round in cross section. Most reports of *A. papillosa* from rocky shores in Britain and Ireland are probably *A. filomenae*.

KEY CHARACTERISTICS Large aeolid with superficial pigment over body and cerata. Usually has a white V on front of head.

Adult amongst the sea anemone *Actinothoe sphyrodeta*, sponges and bryozoans, Portrush, Northern Ireland.

Studio shot of adult, Strangford Lough, Northern Ireland.

Ribbon of spawn surrounding siphons of the sea squirt *Polycarpa* sp., Portrush, Northern Ireland.

Aeolidia papillosa (Linnaeus, 1761)

DESCRIPTION This is the largest aeolid in Britain and Ireland, reaching 120 mm in length. It is usually grey in overall appearance due to freckles of grey or brown pigment, but the colour is very variable. The oral tentacles and rhinophores are tapering with thick bases. The cerata are round in cross section. The spawn is distinctive, consisting of a thread coiled back and forth and laid in a spiral.

ECOLOGY *Aeolidia papillosa* feeds on sea anemones, primarily *Metridium senile.*

DISTRIBUTION This species has been reported from around Britain and Ireland, northern and southern Europe, the Atlantic coast of North America and Alaska. It is a cold-water species, and records from Atlantic Spain and France are likely to be *Aeolidia filomenae* while it becomes more common in Norway, Denmark and the Netherlands.

SIMILAR SPECIES *A. papillosa* was recently revised and an additional two species were established, *Aeolidia filomenae* (p. 310) and *Aeolidia loui* from California. Unlike *A. filomenae, A. papillosa* is usually found sublittorally and lacks the white V-shaped pigment on the head.

KEY CHARACTERISTICS Large aeolid with superficial pigment over body and cerata. Head with mottled brown pigment.

One individual nestled amongst the sea anemone *Metridium senile*, Connemara, Ireland.

Studio shot of adult, Belfast Lough, Northern Ireland.

Spawn coil on bedrock, Rathlin Island, Northern Ireland.

Aeolidiella alderi

(Cocks, 1852)

DESCRIPTION This nudibranch has a pale fawn coloration with some superficial orange pigment on the dorsum. The numerous cerata have white cnidosacs which are particularly large in the anterior cluster, giving a white collar or 'ruff' to the animal. There is little surface pigment on the ceratal surfaces, allowing the grey or dark grey digestive gland to be clearly seen. The rhinophores have paler pigment increasing in density towards the tips. The spawn is a convoluted spiral thread containing large eggs.

ECOLOGY This is an intertidal species which feeds on a variety of sea anemones, particularly *Cereus pedunculatus*, *Diadumene cincta* and *Cylista elegans*. It has direct development with no veliger larval stage.

DISTRIBUTION Found only in the south and west of Britain and Ireland, with a few records from western Ireland. This species extends along the south coast of England to the Isle of Wight and the Medina Estuary. On the French Atlantic coast, it is frequent but sporadic in occurrence. It is also found in the Mediterranean Sea.

SIMILAR SPECIES Possible confusion with *Aeolidiella glauca* (p. 316), *A.* cf. *glauca* (p. 318) and *A. sanguinea* (p. 320). *Aeolidiella alderi* can usually be distinguished by the white 'ruff' and it often has some orange pigment at the tips of the rhinophores.

KEY CHARACTERISTICS Body with sparse superficial pigment. First cluster of cerata with elongated cnidosacs giving white 'ruff'.

Individual under a rock, Mediterranean coast of Spain. (Enric Madrenas)

Studio shot of adult, Plymouth, England. (David Fenwick)

Adult with spawn, Mediterranean coast of Spain. (Enric Madrenas)

Aeolidiella glauca (Alder & Hancock, 1845)

DESCRIPTION The body of this nudibranch is orange-brown in colour with extensive fawn or light brown surface pigment on the dorsum and in a rim around the edge of the foot. Some individuals are bright red and can be confused with *Aeolidiella sanguinea*. The cerata are covered with dense flecks of fawn coloured pigment. The outer half of the oral tentacles and rhinophores are similarly pigmented. The spawn is a smoothly coiled thread with distinct breaks at regular intervals.

ECOLOGY Typically, a sublittoral species in exposed or current-swept rocky sites, but occasionally found on the lower shore. This species feeds on sagartiid anemones, especially *Cylista elegans*. Probably more active at night and hiding beneath rocks or in dark overhanging crevices in the daytime.

DISTRIBUTION Widely distributed around the British coasts, in tidal streams and on exposed rocky coasts. Present throughout Norway but becomes increasingly rare to the south of France. Scarce and usually found in small numbers.

SIMILAR SPECIES All *Aeolidiella* species are quite variable in colour, becoming more pigmented as they grow larger and with their ceratal contents often coloured by the anemones they have eaten. Very similar to *Aeolidiella* cf. *glauca* (p. 318) but usually more brightly pigmented. *Aeolidiella alderi* (p. 314) and *A. sanguinea* (p. 320) are also hard to distinguish from this species.

KEY CHARACTERISTICS Superficial pigment on ceratal surfaces and around edge of foot. Rhinophores and oral tentacles with outer portion pigmented.

Adult with the sea anemone *Cylista elegans*, Bodø, Norway.

Studio shot of adult, Strangford Lough, Northern Ireland.

Spiral of spawn on silty rock, West Cork, Ireland.

Aeolidiella cf. *glauca* (Alder & Hancock, 1845)

DNA sequence data indicate substantial differences with *Aeolidiella glauca*.

DESCRIPTION The body of this nudibranch is pale pink in colour with extensive fawn or light brown surface pigment on the dorsum and in a rim around the edge of the foot. The cerata are covered with dense flecks of fawn coloured pigment. The outer half of the oral tentacles and rhinophores are similarly pigmented. The spawn is a smoothly coiled thread with distinct breaks at regular intervals.

ECOLOGY A sublittoral species feeding on sagartiid anemones, especially *Cylista lacerata*. This anemone is usually found in sheltered muddy sites attached to pieces of shell or small stones embedded in mud.

DISTRIBUTION Widely distributed around the British coasts, in muddy inlets such as Strangford Lough, but also on exposed rocky coasts. Further distribution includes the Netherlands and Norway. Scarce and usually found in small numbers.

SIMILAR SPECIES Currently confused with *A. glauca* (p. 316) but found in sheltered muddy habitats where *Cylista lacerata* is present.

KEY CHARACTERISTICS Superficial pigment on ceratal surfaces and around edge of foot. Rhinophores and oral tentacles with outer portion pigmented.

Adult on muddy sand, Strangford Lough, Northern Ireland.

Studio shot of adult, Zeeland, Netherlands.

Adult and spawn on sea squirt, Strangford Lough, Ireland.

Aeolidiella sanguinea (Norman, 1877)

DESCRIPTION The cerata of this nudibranch are short and neatly arranged. The entire body and cerata are usually pale to bright red in colour, but occasional brown or greenish brown individuals have been reported; the colour is probably influenced by diet. The rhinophores have conspicuous white tips which are clearly differentiated from the rest of the rhinophore. The oral tentacles and cerata also have white tips. The spawn is a spiral thread with scalloped sections separated by breaks.

ECOLOGY A rather scarce species in Britain and Ireland, usually found beneath rocks in the intertidal, but occasionally in the sublittoral. This species has large eyes and is more active at night, at least in captivity. It feeds on sagartiid anemones, especially on *Cylista elegans*.

DISTRIBUTION Recorded from the western coasts of Britain and Ireland, the Atlantic coasts of France, Spain, and Portugal.

SIMILAR SPECIES Some intertidal individuals of *Aeolidiella glauca* (p. 316) and *Aeolidiella alderi* (p. 314) have extensive bright orange pigmentation and could be confused with this species.

KEY CHARACTERISTICS Red coloration throughout body with little surface pigment. Conspicuous well-defined white tips to the rhinophores.

Studio shot of pale-coloured individual, Galway, Ireland.

Studio shot of adult, Salt Lake, Clifden, Connemara, Ireland.

Studio shot of adult, Connemara, Ireland.

Berghia norvegica

Odhner, 1939

DESCRIPTION *Berghia* species have distinctive rhinophores covered with rounded papillae. *Berghia norvegica* is translucent white in colour with no surface pigment. It has tapering rhinophores and the oral tentacles have slightly roughened surfaces. The cerata have an orange-pink hue and the digestive gland and cnidosacs are clearly visible within. Maximum size is about 30 mm. The spawn is a broad spiral thread with sections separated by small breaks.

ECOLOGY This species is usually found below 25 m depth and is more active at night, often hiding beneath stones during the daytime. It feeds on the tiny pink anemone *Gonactinia prolifera*.

DISTRIBUTION Currently only known from a few locations in Norway, from the Trondheim Fjord where it was first found, south to the Sogn Fjord.

SIMILAR SPECIES Similar in overall appearance to *Aeolidiella* species (pp. 314–320) but the papillate rhinophores are very distinctive.

KEY CHARACTERISTICS Translucent white with pink-orange hue throughout the cerata. Rhinophores tapering with rounded warts covering all surfaces.

On coralline encrusted bedrock with the anemone *Gonactinia prolifera*, Gulen, Norway.

Studio shot of adult, Gulen, Norway.

Spawn coil on underside of a *Modiolus* shell, Gulen, Norway.

Berghia coerulescens (Laurillard, 1832)

DESCRIPTION A relatively large aeolid 40–70 mm in length; the body is translucent greyish white. The oral tentacles and papillate rhinophores are bright orange and there are 2 orange lines in front of the rhinophores. The spindle-shaped cerata are blue with yellow-orange tips.

ECOLOGY Occurs on the low shore and shallow subtidal where it feeds on sea anemones such as *Aiptasia couchii*.

DISTRIBUTION Originally described from Nice on the French Mediterranean coast. Recorded from St Malo on the north coast of France 100 years ago, this species has recently been found in small numbers in the Channel Isles. Reported from Atlantic coasts of France, Spain, Portugal, and the Mediterranean Sea.

SIMILAR SPECIES This brightly coloured species is unmistakeable.

KEY CHARACTERISTICS Orange papillate rhinophores. Orange stripes on head. Blue cerata with yellow tips.

Adult on coralline encrusted bedrock, Écréhous, Channel Islands. (Nicolas Joault)

Smaller individual from Mediterranean coast of Spain. (Enric Madrenas)

Adult and spawn, Écréhous, Channel Islands. (Nicolas Joault)

Cerberilla bernadettae

Tardy, 1960

DESCRIPTION *Cerberilla* species have a very broad foot and long sweeping oral tentacles held out to the sides of the head. *Cerberilla bernadettae* is translucent white with a brown hue to the spindle-shaped cerata. The rhinophores are short and smooth and held erect. The eyes are large, positioned below the rhinophores. There is a curved dark brown line wrapped around the side of the head from behind the oral tentacle which runs behind the rhinophore and along the back. The tip of each ceras has a triangular dark brown mark on the upper surface. The rhinophores, oral tentacles and the long foot-corners are translucent brown, and a diffuse white stripe runs along the top of the oral tentacles.

ECOLOGY Occurs on sandy seabeds where it searches across the surface for burrowing sea anemones. It can burrow quickly into the sand.

DISTRIBUTION Recorded from Brittany south to the Mediterranean Sea.

SIMILAR SPECIES *Cerberilla* cf. *bernadettae*, illustrated here, differs in having orange rhinophores, orange tips to the oral tentacles and no orange spot at the tip of the cerata. Garcia-Gómez (2002) illustrates the true *C. bernadettae* and the type locality is Brittany. Cattaneo-Vietti *et al.* (1990) and Trainito & Doneddu (2014) illustrate *C.* cf. *bernadettae*, which is recorded from as far west as Granada in Spain.

KEY CHARACTERISTICS Long oral tentacles. Head with distinctive brown markings. Brown marks on cerata.

Cerberilla bernadettae with brown rhinophores and oral tentacles, on sand, Sepieres, L'Escala. (Enric Madrenas)

Cerberilla cf. *bernadettae* on sand, Cagnes-sur-Mer, France. (Xavier Rufray)

Cerberilla cf. *bernadettae* on sand, Cagnes-sur-Mer, France. (Xavier Rufray)

Acteon tornatilis

(Linnaeus, 1758)

DESCRIPTION The family Acteonidae are heterobranch gastropods with a solid external shell which looks like the shell of other gastropod groups. The body is translucent white and can retract completely into the shell. Typically, 12–30 mm in length.

ECOLOGY This species lives at the surface of sand and can burrow into the sand. It feeds on polychaetes such as *Owenia fusiformis*.

DISTRIBUTION Found from low water to 250 m depth on sandy seabeds around Britain and Ireland and from Iceland and Norway to the Mediterranean Sea.

SIMILAR SPECIES There are no similar species in the area, but currently 69 species of *Acteon* worldwide.

KEY CHARACTERISTICS Thin shell with short spire and brown bands. White animal with broad foot.

Semi-buried in sand, Rathlin Island, Northern Ireland.

Studio shot, Rathlin Island, Northern Ireland.

Studio shot, Rathlin Island, Northern Ireland.

Scaphander lignarius (Linnaeus, 1758)

DESCRIPTION Also known as the Canoe Shell or Woody Canoe Shell, the name *lignarius* refers to the shell's resemblance to wood grain. The shell varies in colour and can be yellow, brown or olive green. The shell can be up to 70 mm in length but is typically 40–55 mm. The shell is ovoid in outline and is much broader at the head end and narrows towards the apex. The edges of the shell curl inwards, hence the name 'canoe' shell. The body is white to yellow in colour and is up to twice the length of the shell. The head is broad and flattened and lacks tentacles. There is a large, flat, parapodial lobe on either side of the foot.

ECOLOGY *Scaphander lignarius* lives in muddy and sandy bottoms where it burrows into the sediment to feed on bivalve shells and polychaete worms. It has been recorded from 5 to 700 m depth.

DISTRIBUTION Reported from around the coasts of Britain and Ireland, north to northern Norway and south into the Mediterranean.

SIMILAR SPECIES There are no other species with a shell of this shape in the area covered by this guide.

KEY CHARACTERISTICS Distinctive shell. Large white body partially concealing the shell.

Semi-buried in shelly sand, Rathlin Island, Northern Ireland.

On shelly sand, Rathlin Island, Northern Ireland.

Shell only, Crinnis Beach, Carlyon Bay, Cornwall. (David Fenwick)

Colpodaspis pusilla

M Sars, 1870

DESCRIPTION A tiny sea slug with an internal shell. The shell is covered by the mantle and there are 2 prominent head tentacles. The tentacles, tail and mantle are coloured with powdery white pigment. At the back right hand side the mantle is extended into a fold which constitutes the exhalant siphon. A posterior pallial lobe of the mantle covers the foot at the rear. This species is 5 mm in length.

ECOLOGY Rocky reefs in strong or moderate tidal streams. Feeds on sea squirts including *Pycnoclavella stolonialis* and possibly other *Pycnoclavella* species.

DISTRIBUTION Rarely found except by divers, originally described from Norway. Regularly found on western coasts of Britain and Ireland and recorded from the western Mediterranean to Norway.

SIMILAR SPECIES The only similar sea slug with white surface pigment is *Laona pruinosa* (p. 337). There are two other tiny sea slugs which are found in rockpools and amongst algae. They are *Runcina coronata* and *Runcina ferruginea* (opposite, below). *Runcina* species have 3 simple gills tucked in between the back of the mantle and the foot (Araujo *et al.*, 2022).

KEY CHARACTERISTICS Small, with circular mantle and 2 head tentacles. Head protruding from under the mantle.

Three individuals on silty bedrock, Sark, Channel Islands.

Studio shot of adult *Colpodaspis pusilla*, Skomer, Wales.

Runcina coronata has characteristic patterns at the head and tail, lower shore on the reef west of Gyllyngvase, Falmouth, Cornwall, England. (David Fenwick)

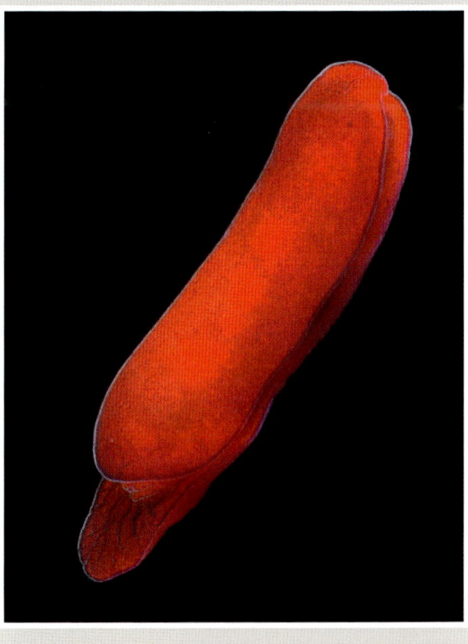

Runcina ferruginea is entirely red in colour. Albert Pier, Penzance, Cornwall, England. (David Fenwick)

Philine quadripartita

Ascanius, 1772

DESCRIPTION Body consists of 5 distinct parts, a head lobe, body, and shell with 2 parapodial lobes to the sides and a tail lobe which is slightly cleft at the tip. *Philine quadripartita* can grow to over 70 mm in length.

ECOLOGY Found on soft mud or sand, crawling at the surface with a mucus covering and burrowing into the mud. Species of *Philine* feed on foraminifera and bivalves which they crush with 3 calcareous gizzard plates.

DISTRIBUTION Atlantic and Mediterranean coasts of Europe and Africa.

SIMILAR SPECIES There are several other species of Philinidae in the area which are smaller. *Laona pruinosa* (p. 337) is 17 mm in length with a translucent white body with white pigmented borders to the parapodial lobes. *Philine scabra* (not included here) has a narrow body and is translucent white and reaches 20 mm in length. The other species are 5–16 mm in length and white, brown or mottled in colour. They are distinguished by the sculpturing of their shells.

KEY CHARACTERISTICS White, flattened slug with the back of the body divided into 5 lobes.

Semi-buried in fine mud, Carlingford Lough, Northern Ireland.

On fine mud, Carlingford Lough, Northern Ireland.

Spawn mass, Connemara, Ireland.

Philine catena (Montagu, 1803)

DESCRIPTION This species has a narrow body with a rectangular head lobe, lateral parapodial lobes and a visceral lobe containing a transparent shell. The surface is pale orange-brown with small, evenly dispersed spots of cream and with darker chestnut brown pigment on the rear part of the head lobe and on the visceral lobe. The shell is decorated with chains of oval transparent markings. The body reaches 10 mm in length.

ECOLOGY Little is known about the ecology of this small animal which can be found in samples collected amongst seaweeds and sessile animals. Philinids are predatory on small molluscs, worms and foraminifera.

DISTRIBUTION *Philine catena* has been recorded from the Lofoten Islands in Norway south to the Mediterranean Sea from the intertidal zone to 2,000 m depth.

SIMILAR SPECIES There are several species of philinids which are not covered in this guide.

KEY CHARACTERISTICS Elongate narrow body. Chain-like shell sculpture.

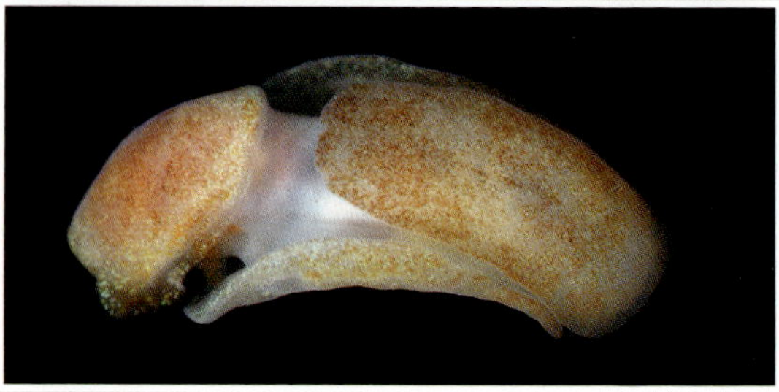

Above: Penzance, Cornwall, England. Below left: Studio shot shell only, Marazion, Cornwall, England. Below right: Studio shot, Marazion, Cornwall, England. (All David Fenwick)

Laona pruinosa (Clark, 1827)

DESCRIPTION The thin, fragile shell is translucent. It is enclosed and hidden by the fused parapodial lobes. Body length to about 15 mm.

ECOLOGY Usually found on coarse, tide-swept, gravel seabeds or more sheltered silty sites. Probably feeds on foraminifera and possibly polychaete worms and small bivalves. Unlike Philinidae species, Laonidae have no gizzard plates.

DISTRIBUTION From Norway, Britain and Ireland, south to the Mediterranean.

SIMILAR SPECIES Smaller than *Philine quadripartita* (p. 334) and with a translucent body with opaque white surface pigment. *Colpodaspis pusilla* (p. 332) is similar in colour but has the head clearly beneath the visceral lobe and no lateral lobes.

KEY CHARACTERISTICS Body with head shield, lateral lobes and visceral mass enclosing shell. Translucent with white pigment spots and white outline to head shield and lateral lobes.

Studio shot, west coast of Scotland.

Haminoea navicula (da Costa, 1778)

DESCRIPTION The thin, fragile, bubble-like shell is pale brown in colour. It is largely hidden by the large parapodial lobes and the posterior pallial lobe. Body length to about 70 mm.

ECOLOGY Usually found in sheltered mud or muddy sand habitats, especially *Zostera* seagrass beds.

DISTRIBUTION Ireland to the Mediterranean.

SIMILAR SPECIES *Akera bullata* (p. 348) is similar in appearance, size, and habitat but the shell is at the end of the body. *Haminoea hydatis* (not included here) has been recorded from the south coast of England. It differs from this species in its much smaller size and the fact that the parapodial lobes are small, leaving most of the shell uncovered.

KEY CHARACTERISTICS Elongate slug with shell in middle of back, mostly hidden by two lateral lobes. Flat shield-like head with tiny eyes.

A swarm of slugs on mud, Valentia Island, Ireland.

Two individuals on fine mud, Connemara, Ireland.

Spawn mass, Connemara, Ireland.

Elysia viridis

(Montagu, 1804)

DESCRIPTION The body colour, green to bright red, is dependent on the colour of the algae it is feeding on. There are usually scattered iridescent red, blue, and green spots, and there can be white patches on the parapodial edges and black markings in the head and elsewhere. Branching ducts and lobes of the digestive gland are visible through the body wall in all parts of the body. Grows to about 45 mm in length but typically 12–15 mm.

ECOLOGY *Elysia viridis* has been reported from a variety of species of alga, but it actually eats the filamentous algae *Cladophora* and *Chaetomorpha* as well as coenocytic algae *Codium* and *Bryopsis*. It is able to retain living plastids from its algal food, allowing the plastids to continue to photosynthesise within its body. The slug's colour is algal-derived, leading to the different colour 'morphs' which have been reported for this species.

DISTRIBUTION Northeast Atlantic from Norway to the Mediterranean.

SIMILAR SPECIES Only one species of *Elysia* is currently known from the region covered here.

KEY CHARACTERISTICS Long, slender bright green body with leaf-like parapodia which wrap around the body.

Amongst red algae, Connemara, Ireland.

Alderia modesta (Lovén, 1844)

DESCRIPTION This is a small sea slug growing to a maximum of 10 mm. The foot is broader than the body and the back of the animal is covered in cerata. The body and cerata are speckled with green, brown and white pigment.

ECOLOGY Usually found in salt marshes or estuaries where is feeds on green algae.

DISTRIBUTION Reported as occurring on both sides of the Atlantic; in Europe this species has been reported from Norway to the Atlantic coast of France.

SIMILAR SPECIES Unlike any other sea slug from the region covered by this book.

KEY CHARACTERISTICS No head tentacles. Cerata on sides of body.

Studio shot, Zeeland, Netherlands.

Calliopaea bellula

d'Orbigny, 1837

DESCRIPTION A tiny sea slug with rounded cerata, growing to 10 mm in length.

ECOLOGY Unlike other sacoglossans which feed by piercing algal cells, this species feeds on the eggs of other sea slugs. It has been observed in numbers on the egg masses of *Philine quadripartita*.

DISTRIBUTION Recorded from Norway to the Mediterranean Sea. Rarely reported but may be common when it is found.

SIMILAR SPECIES There are three other tiny black sea slugs which are quite common but rarely seen because they are so small. They are usually about 5 mm in length. They are *Limapontia capitata* (opposite), which is a rockpool dweller feeding on the green alga *Cladophora* spp., *Limapontia senestra* (opposite, below), which is often in the same rockpools, and *Limapontia depressa* (opposite) which lives on saltmarshes with *Alderia modesta* (p. 341). *Runcina coronata* (p. 333) can also be found in clean rockpools with coralline algae.

Calliopaea bellula, studio shot, Strangford Lough, County Down, Ireland.

Limapontia capitata on the green alga *Cladophora rupestris*, Penzance, Cornwall. (David Fenwick)

Limapontia senestra studio shot, Challaborough, Devon, England. (David Fenwick)

Limapontia depressa studio shot, The Skern, Westward Ho!, Devon, England. (David Fenwick)

Placida dendritica

(Alder & Hancock, 1843)

DESCRIPTION This is a small sea slug; adults are usually between 5 and 8 mm in length. The body is translucent white in colour, and green digestive gland is visible through the body and particularly conspicuous in the cerata. The tips of the cerata and rhinophores are speckled with white pigment.

ECOLOGY Feeds on green algae such as *Codium fragile* and *Bryopsis plumosa*.

DISTRIBUTION This species has been reported as having a cosmopolitan distribution, but it is likely that the records represent a species complex.

SIMILAR SPECIES Sacoglossans are sometimes mistaken for nudibranchs, but careful examination of this species reveals rhinophores which are inrolled, like a cylinder open down one side.

Studio shot, Carrickfergus Marina, County Down, Ireland.

Hermaea bifida (Montagu, 1815)

DESCRIPTION A small sea slug which can be up to 24 mm in length. The body is semi-transparent, and internal organs such as the cerebral ganglia, reproductive and digestive organs are clearly visible. A conspicuous, reddish brown duct of digestive gland runs down either side of the body and branches into each of the cerata. The animals have a strong, characteristic smell if they are in a container of seaweed.

ECOLOGY Feeds on red algae such as *Griffithsia flosculosa* which gives it the reddish brown colour.

DISTRIBUTION Although this species has been reported from around Britain and Ireland, Norway, Iberian Peninsula, and the western Mediterranean, some of the more southern records may well be attributed to the recently described *Hermaea cantabra* Caballer & Ortea, 2015.

SIMILAR SPECIES *Hermaea cantabra*, *Hermaea paucicirra* and *Hermaea variopicta* (see pp. 346–347) have all been reported from northwest Europe as far north as Cornwall, and for *H. variopicta* southeast Ireland.

Hermaea bifida amongst brown seaweed, Connemara, Ireland.

Hermaea bifida studio shot, Connemara, Ireland.

Hermaea paucicirra, studio shot, Newlyn, Cornwall, England. (David Fenwick)

Hermaea cantabra, studio shot, Newlyn, Cornwall, England. (David Fenwick)

Hermaea variopicta, Ille-et-Vilaine, Brittany, France. (Pierre Corbrion)

Akera bullata

Muller, 1776

DESCRIPTION *Akera bullata* is a sea hare with a bubble-shaped external shell, an elongated neck and head region, and parapodia which fold over on each side to partially enclose the body. The shell is at the tail end of the body. 50–80 mm in length.

ECOLOGY Normally crawling or burrowing in mud, sand or gravel in the shallow infralittoral on sheltered shores. At times they form swimming swarms, often in quite large numbers. They swim by vigorously flapping the parapodia with their heavy (shelled) end hanging down.

DISTRIBUTION Known from northeast Atlantic coasts of Europe and the Mediterranean. Usually in sheltered sites and even in marinas.

SIMILAR SPECIES *Haminoea navicula* (p. 338) is superficially similar but has the shell in the middle of the back with a rounded tail behind.

KEY CHARACTERISTICS Bubble shell extending beyond the pallial lobes above the tail. Pallial lobes overlapping across the back.

On muddy maerl, Connemara, Ireland.

Adult swimming, Connemara, Ireland.

Two individuals and spawn, Connemara, Ireland.

Aplysia punctata

Cuvier, 1803

DESCRIPTION Grows up to 20 cm. Body colour variable, ranging from olive green to brown, red or purplish black, with blotches of grey, white, often with black or dark brown spots and veining. The body is long and narrow and the parapodia join rather high posteriorly.

ECOLOGY Amongst algae on the lower shore and in shallow water to the limit of algal growth. The colour often matches the predominant algae in the area, from red to brown to green.

DISTRIBUTION Northeast Atlantic from Greenland to Mediterranean.

SIMILAR SPECIES Two larger sea hares occur occasionally in southern England. They are *Aplysia depilans* and *Aplysia fasciata* (not included here).

KEY CHARACTERISTICS Head shape with rolled tentacles. Back with 2 folds enclosing thin shell.

A red individual on the red seaweed *Odonthalia dentata*, Rathlin Island, Northern Ireland.

Studio shot of adult, Rathlin Island, Northern Ireland.

A tangle of spawn on the red seaweed *Delesseria sanguinea*, the Maidens, Northern Ireland.

Berthella plumula (Montagu, 1803)

DESCRIPTION The thin, transparent shell is internal and is about half the body length, which may reach about 60 mm. Pale lemon yellow to orange in colour, often with net-like markings in the middle of the smooth dorsal mantle. A gill is present on the right-hand side of the body, concealed between the mantle and the foot. The skin can secrete defensive sulphuric acid if attacked.

ECOLOGY Feeds on the sponge *Oscarella* sp. (the *Oscarella* in Britain and Ireland is probably not named and is distinct from Mediterranean *O. lobularis*). The appearance of *Berthella plumula* seems to be providing camouflage on *Oscarella*, with a central transparent patch mimicking an oscule of the sponge and the reticulate pattern looking similar to lobules of the sponge.

DISTRIBUTION A common species around Britain and Ireland and extending from Norway to the Mediterranean. Normally found beneath rocks on the lower shore but also frequent at St. Kilda on the west coast of Scotland down to depths of 30 m on steep rock faces.

SIMILAR SPECIES *Berthellina citrina* (not included here) has been reported from the UK, but it is more likely that these records refer to *Berthellina edwardsii* (opposite, below) or possibly *Berthellina aurantiaca* (not included here).

KEY CHARACTERISTICS Mantle extends over the head and rhinophore bases. *Berthella* with yellow mantle and characteristic mottling. *Berthellina* with orange coloration and no markings.

On sheltered bedrock with spirorbid worms, Strangford Lough, Northern Ireland.

Studio shot of adult, Connemara, Ireland.

Berthellina edwardsii beneath a rock, L'Escala, Girona, Spain. (Enric Madrenas)

Pleurobranchus membranaceus (Montagu, 1815)

DESCRIPTION A large sea slug normally found in sheltered areas where the sea squirt *Ascidiella aspersa* is present. There are soft, pointed tubercles all over the back, and the rhinophores and oral tentacles extend from under the front of the mantle. The body is translucent reddish brown in colour and protrudes below a mantle which has a mottled appearance. The colour consists of spots of opaque white pigment which coalesce into patches between the tubercles. The edge of the foot also has irregular white spots. There is often some silt collected on the back, increasing the camouflage effect. There is a large gill in the space between the mantle and the foot on the right-hand side of the body. Grows to 120 mm in length.

ECOLOGY Feeds on simple and compound ascidians, especially *Ascidiella aspersa*. *Pleurobranchus membranaceus* swims upside down with an asynchronous flapping of the foot. The mantle hangs down and is not used in swimming, while the sides of the foot extend out as large thin flaps, much larger than when the animal is crawling. During swimming the foot on one side performs a swimming stroke by sending a wave from the front to rear and then while it is recovering for the next propulsive stroke, the other side of the foot undergoes its propulsive stroke. This makes swimming a very ungainly unstable movement, the animal rolling from side to side as it swims along. Animals do not appear to swim in any direction.

DISTRIBUTION A common species around Britain and Ireland and extending from Norway to the Mediterranean Sea.

Adult on shelly mud, Connemara, Ireland.

Adult laying spawn, Connemara, Ireland.

Distinctive spawn coil, Connemara, Ireland.

References

Araujo, A. K., Pola, M., Malaquias, M. A. E., Ballesteros, M., Vitale, F. & Cervera, J. L. (2022). Molecular phylogeny of European Runcinida (Gastropoda, Heterobranchia): the discovery of an unexpected pool of complex species, with special reference to the case of *Runcina coronata*. *Zoological Journal of the Linnean Society.* 194(3): 761–788.

Ekimova, I., Korshunova, T., Schepetov, D., Neretina, T., Sanamyan, N. & Martynov, A. V. (2015). Integrative systematics of northern and Arctic nudibranchs of the genus *Dendronotus* (Mollusca, Gastropoda), with descriptions of three new species. *Zoological Journal of the Linnean Society.* 173(4): 841–886.

Furfaro G. & Trainito E. (2017). A new species from the Mediterranean Sea and North-Eastern Atlantic Ocean: *Knoutsodonta pictoni* n. sp. (Gastropoda Heterobranchia Nudibranchia). *Biodiversity Journal.* 8(2): 725–738.

Furfaro, G., Mariottini, P., Modica, M. V., Trainito, E., Doneddu, M. & Oliverio, M. (2016a). Sympatric sibling species: the case of *Caloria elegans* and *Facelina quatrefagesi* (Gastropoda: Nudibranchia). *Scientia Marina.* 80(4): 511.

Furfaro, G., Picton, B., Martynov, A. & Mariottini, P. (2016b). *Diaphorodoris alba* Portmann & Sandmeier, 1960 is a valid species: molecular and morphological comparison with *D. luteocincta* (M. Sars, 1870) (Gastropoda: Nudibranchia). *Zootaxa.* 4193(2): 304–316.

Korshunova, T., Bakken, T., Grøtan, V. V., Johnson, K. B., Lundin, K. & Martynov, A. (2020a). A synoptic review of the family Dendronotidae (Mollusca: Nudibranchia): a multilevel organismal diversity approach. *Contributions to Zoology.* 90(1): 93–153.

Korshunova, T. A., Driessen, F. M. F., Picton, B. E. & Martynov, A. (2021). The multilevel organismal diversity approach deciphers difficult to distinguish nudibranch species complex. *Scientific Reports.* 11(1).

Korshunova, T., Lundin, K., Malmberg, K. & Martynov, A. (2023). Narrowly defined taxa on a global scale: The phylogeny and taxonomy of the genera *Catriona* and *Tenellia* (Nudibranchia, Trinchesiidae) favours fine-scale taxonomic differentiation and dissolution of the 'lumpers & splitters' dilemma. *Evolutionary Applications.*

Korshunova, T., Lundin, K., Malmberg, K., Picton, B. & Martynov, A. (2018). First true brackish-water nudibranch mollusc provides new insights for phylogeny and biogeography and reveals paedomorphosis-driven evolution. *PLOS ONE.* 13(3): e0192177.

Korshunova, T., Malmberg, K., Prkić, J., Petani, A., Fletcher, K., Lundin, K. & Martynov, A. (2020b). Fine-scale species delimitation: speciation in process and periodic patterns in nudibranch diversity. *ZooKeys.* 917: 15–50.

Korshunova, T. & Martynov, A. (2020). Consolidated data on the phylogeny and evolution of the family Tritoniidae (Gastropoda: Nudibranchia) contribute to genera reassessment and clarify the taxonomic status of the neuroscience models *Tritonia* and *Tochuina*. *PLOS ONE.* 15(11): e0242103.

Korshunova, T., Martynov, A., Bakken, T., Evertsen, J., Fletcher, K., Mudianta, W., Saito, H., Lundin, K., Schrödl, M. & Picton, B. (2017a). Polyphyly of the traditional family Flabellinidae affects a major group of Nudibranchia: aeolidacean taxonomic reassessment with descriptions of several new families, genera, and species (Mollusca, Gastropoda). *ZooKeys.* 717: 1–139.

Korshunova, T., Martynov, A., Bakken, T. & Picton, B. (2017b). External diversity is restrained by internal conservatism: new nudibranch mollusc contributes to the cryptic species problem. *Zoologica Scripta.* DOI: 10.1111/zsc.12253.

Korshunova, T., Martynov, A. & Picton, B. (2017c). Ontogeny as an important part of integrative taxonomy in tergipedid aeolidaceans (Gastropoda: Nudibranchia) with a description of a new genus and species from the Barents Sea. *Zootaxa.* 4324(1): 1.

Korshunova, T., Picton, B., Furfaro, G., Mariottini, P., Pontes, M., Prkić, J., Fletcher, K., Malmberg, K., Lundin, K. & Martynov, A. (2019). Multilevel fine-scale diversity challenges the 'cryptic species' concept. *Scientific Reports.* 9(1).

Neuhaus, J., Rauch, C., Bakken, T., Picton, B., Pola, M. & Malaquias, M. A. E. (2021). The genus *Jorunna* (Nudibranchia: Discodorididae) in Europe: a new species and a possible case of incipient speciation. *Journal of Molluscan Studies.* 87(4).

Sørensen, C. G., Rauch, C., Pola, M. & Malaquias, M. A. E. (2020). Integrative taxonomy reveals a cryptic species of the nudibranch genus *Polycera* (Polyceridae) in European waters. *Journal of the Marine Biological Association of the United Kingdom.* DOI: 10.1017/s0025315420000612, pp. 1-20.

Books on nudibranchs and other sea slugs

Behrens, D. W., Fletcher, K., Hermosillo, A. & Jensen, G. C. (2022). *Nudibranchs & Sea Slugs of the Eastern Pacific.* Mola Marine. 170pp. ISBN: 9780989839129.

Calado, G. & Silva, J. P. (2012). *Sea Slugs of the Algarve – Opisthobranch Guide for the Southern Coast of Portugal.* Edições SubNauta. 164pp. ISBN: 978989964067.

Cattaneo-Vietti, R., Chemello, R. & Giannuzzi-Savelli, R. (eds.), (1990). *Atlas of Mediterranean Nudibranchs.* Editrice La Conchiglia, 264 pp.

Garcia-Gómez, J. C. (2002). *Paradigmas de una fauna insolita: los moluscos opistobranquios del estrecho de Gilbraltar: morfoanatomia y taxonomia de los cefalaspideos, sacoglosos y nudibranquios del estrecho de Gilbraltar y areas proximas.* CEPSA Sultural. 397pp. ISBN: 8488556160, 9788488556165.

Malmberg, K. & Lundin, K. (2015). *Svenska Näkensnäckor.* Waterglobe Productions, 128pp. ISBN: 9789198039474.

Just, H., Edmunds, M. & Platts, E. (1985). *North Atlantic nudibranchs (Mollusca) seen by Henning Lemche with additional species from the Mediterranean and the North East Pacific. Appendix: an annotated list of the North Atlantic Opisthobranchia.* Ophelia. *Supplementum, 2.* Ophelia Publications. 170pp. ISBN 9788798106616.

Thompson, T. E. (1988). *Molluscs: Benthic Opisthobranchs (Mollusca : Gastropoda : Keys and Notes for the Identification of the Species).* 356pp. The Bath Press. ISBN 9789004084391.

Thompson, T. E. & Brown, G. H. (1984). *Biology of Opisthobranch Molluscs, Volume 2.* Ray Society. 229pp. ISBN: 9780903874182.

Trainito, E. & Doneddu, M. (2014). *Nudibranchi del Mediterraneo.* Il Castello. 192pp. ISBN: 9788865204801

Valdés, A., Hamann, J., Behrens, D. W. & DuPont, A. (2006). *Caribbean Sea Slugs: A field guide to the opisthobranch molluscs from the tropical northwestern Atlantic.* Sea Challengers. 289pp. ISBN: 9780970057426.

Yonow, N. (2008). *Sea Slugs of the Red Sea.* Pensoft Publishers. 304pp. ISBN: 9789546423276.

Index

Page numbers in ***bold italic*** refer to main species entries.